# Classroom Instruction and Students With Autism Spectrum Disorders

## A Collection of Articles

From *TEACHING Exceptional Children*

Alec F. Peck and Stan Scarpati
*Editors*

**Council for Exceptional Children**
The voice and vision of special education

ISBN 0-86586-466-7

Printed in the United States of America

10  9  8  7  6  5  4  3  2  1

# Contents

# Acknowledgments

The Council for Exceptional Children would like to extend a special thank you to Alec Peck and Stan Scarpati for their continuing contribution to the field. It is under their leadership that these articles were selected and brought forth to be published in *TEACHING Exceptional Children*.

# Introduction

*Alec F. Peck and Stan Scarpati*

It is readily apparent that the incidence of autism spectrum disorders (ASD) among school-aged students has been accelerating over the past decade. New schools and programs dedicated to serving this population have been built by and for many school districts throughout the United States. Some data indicate that as many as 1 in 91 individuals are affected by one form of the disorder (Kogan et al., 2009). Other statistics suggest that the overall prevalence rate is increasing from 10% to 17% annually, with boys more likely to receive the diagnosis at a rate of four times that of girls (Rice et al., 2007). The dramatic rise can be explained in a variety of ways and is most likely a function of better diagnostic criteria and methods, a wider range of conditions being categorized as ASD, and a higher incidence of autism in the general population. In terms of the more than 100,000 students with ASD receiving services under the Individuals with Disabilities Education Act (IDEA) the number of children diagnosed with autism has grown at a higher rate than any other low-incidence disability category.

These developmental disorders may appear at birth or arise within the first 3 years and may have been diagnosed as pervasive developmental disorders, Asperger's syndrome, Rett syndrome, or childhood disintegrative disorder. Although type and severity level vary across the syndrome, children diagnosed with ASD are generally identified by deficits in their social interaction and in their verbal and nonverbal communication, and repetitive and unusual behaviors or interests.

## EDUCATION PROGRAMS FOR STUDENTS WITH ASD

Although specific causes of ASD are difficult to identify, it is generally agreed that early intervention built on integrative services and parent involvement offers the best opportunity for positive treatment outcomes. Classroom instruction, effective curriculum models, and integrated general and special education programs that evolve from well-designed individualized education programs (IEPs) have played vital roles in the progress of students with ASD.

The National Research Council (Lord & McGee, 2001) reported that the key features of effective education for students with ASD are:

(1) Programs that start as soon as a diagnosis is made,

(2) Intensive instruction based on full-day school programs,

(3) Repeated instruction that is organized around focused one-on-one or small group lessons of short duration anchored by observable and measurable objectives,

(4) A strong family component, and

(5) Procedures that allow for ongoing data collection that provide useful measures of progress as well as program adjustment.

More specifically, educational objectives for children with ASD should include: social skills development; verbal language, receptive language, and nonverbal communication skills; a functional symbolic communication system; engagement and flexibility in developmentally appropriate tasks and play; fine and gross motor skills; cognitive skills (symbolic play and academic skills); development of conventional/appropriate behaviors; and independent organizational skills and skills for success in the general education classroom setting (Lord & McGee, 2001).

## CHARACTERISTICS OF STUDENTS WITH ASD AS LEARNERS

At a general learning level, students with ASD struggle to keep pace with their peers, and specific learning strategies must be shaped to meet their individual needs. For example, it has been shown that students with ASD tend to learn best when information is presented visually using predictable routines and expectations; information should be carefully presented and controlled whenever possible. At times, visual and auditory input may overstimulate students or they may be distracted or overwhelmed by sounds, lights, or images that cannot be properly managed.

To address the common symptom of limited communication skills, some students with ASD benefit from augmentative communication aids and devices such as picture exchange systems that enable students to express concepts and identify objects. The long-standing project TEACCH (Treatment and Education of Autistic and Communication related handicapped CHildren), based at the University of North Carolina-Chapel Hill, for example, utilizes a structured physical and social environment with visual supports so that the child can more easily predict and understand daily activities and respond in appropriate ways.

In addition, many instructional programs are built on the concepts and procedures derived from the direct instruction model. Direct instruction approaches are successful due to their focus on measurable outcomes that are based on a sequence of skills taught along a developmental continuum.

## CLASSROOM INTERVENTIONS AND APPROACHES

This is the second of two collections of articles focused on practical aspects of working with children with ASD and their families. For this publication, we have selected articles from past volumes of *TEACHING Exceptional Children* that focus on classroom instruction and students with ASD. The selection demonstrates a variety of instruction and instruction-related techniques, and represents an evidence-based approach for working with students with ASD. Although the range and type of classroom interventions vary widely—and although some techniques are not yet supported by a substantial body of research evidence—these articles share useful techniques based with valid underpinnings and sufficient clinical validity. The articles we've selected for this volume provide useful information that will assist in bringing high-quality instruction to students with ASD.

This volume begins with "Research-Based Educational Practices for Students With Autism Spectrum Disorders" by Ryan, Hughes, Katsiyannis, McDaniel, and Sprinkle. This article describes in limited detail several of the most popular research-based educational practices for teaching students with ASD, and establishes a well-developed framework within which to better understand the remaining articles. Among the approaches the authors discuss are applied behavior analysis (ABA); the developmental, individual-difference, relationship-based (DIR) approach/Floortime (Wieder & Greenspan, 2001); the Picture Exchange Communication system (PECS; Bondy & Frost, 1994); social stories (Gray & Garand, 1993); and TEACCH (Schopler & Reichler, 1971).

## CURRICULUM AND INSTRUCTION

Following the lead article, Goodman and Williams address the complex issue of keeping students with autism engaged academically and socially. In "Interventions for Increasing the Academic Engagement of Students With Autism Spectrum Disorders in Inclusive Classrooms," they present a series of strategies that focus on the intersection of auditory, visual, social, and physical activities. They emphasize that these strategies are most effective when used in combination and are tailored to the individual characteristics of the learner and the task.

Engaging academic tasks and maintaining independent functioning is the focus of "Using Structured Work Systems to Promote Independence and Engagement for Students With Autism Spectrum Disorders" by Carnahan, Hume, Clarke, and Borders. They highlight practical strategies for designing and implementing structured work systems using visual techniques, which respond to students' selective attention, organization and sequencing, initiation, and generalization cognitive difficulties.

In a similar vein, Falk-Ross, Iverson, and Gilbert, in "Teaching and Learning Approaches for Children With Asperger's Syndrome: Literacy Implications and Applications," link these students' characteristics to the literacy and language demands of a middle school curriculum, and identify research-based interventions that can be implemented in integrated settings. Falk-Ross and colleagues include sample case studies to demonstrate how to implement these coordinated interventions.

Related to this approach to literacy instruction, Susan E. Gately, in "Facilitating Reading Comprehension for Students on the Autism Spectrum," draws attention to strategies that incorporate visual aids such as color and graphics, and provides concrete ways of thinking about narrative texts. In addition, she describes activities and steps to follow when including background knowledge, think-aloud protocols, explicit teaching of story structure, and teaching about characters' emotions.

For mathematics, Donaldson and Zager illustrate the similarities between students with ASD and students with nonverbal learning disabilities when mathematics instruction is matched to student difficulties in cognition and language. In their article, "Mathematics Interventions for Students With High Functioning Autism/Asperger's Syndrome," they present ways to better implement diagnoses for both groups as well as related structured interventions.

## SUPPORTING INSTRUCTION AND LEARNING

The next series of articles demonstrate that instruction can often be facilitated with unique techniques that take advantage of the positive cognitive and linguistic characteristics of students with ASD. Creative classroom-based approaches are the hallmark of these articles and they demonstrate that individualized instruction can be buttressed by research-based ancillary practices.

Two articles focus on the visual strengths of students with ASD. In the first, "Using Visual Script Interventions to Address Communication Skills," Jennifer Ganz suggests that visual cues along with scripts can be useful additions to learning activities. She provides examples of visual scripts and how they may be implemented. Banda, Matuszny, and Turkan discuss "Video Modeling Strategies to Enhance Appropriate Behaviors in Children With Autism Spectrum Disorders." After a review of the literature on video modeling and highlighting precautions that teachers must consider when using these interventions, the authors present a step-by-step approach for employing the video modeling strategy in classroom/therapy settings.

Finally, Banda, Grimmett, and Hart, in "Activity Schedules: Helping Students With Autism Spectrum Disorders in General Education Classrooms Manage Transition Issues," present activity schedules that facilitate transition in and between class routines. They include steps to construct and implement an activity schedule in the general education/inclusive classroom and a brief review of the literature on activity schedules with children with ASD.

We sincerely believe that careful reading and careful, faithful implementation of the techniques described in this volume will be of great value to both the teachers of students with ASD and to the students themselves. Especially when read in tandem with the companion volume of this series, which focuses on students with ASD in the home and community at large, the articles presented here represent some of the best of *TEACHING Exceptional Children* over the past 10 years.

# REFERENCES

Bondy, A. S., & Frost, L. (1994) The picture exchange communication system. *Focus on Autistic Behavior, 9,* 1–19.

Gray, C. A., & Garand, J. D. (1993). Social stories. Improving responses of students with autism with accurate social information. *Focus on Autistic Behavior, 8,* 1–10.

Kogan, M. D., Blumberg, S. J., Schieve, L. A., Boyle, C. A., Perrin, J. M., Ghandour, R. M., . . . Van Dyck, P. C. (2009). Prevalence of parent-reported diagnosis of autism spectrum disorder among children in the US, 2007. *Pediatrics, 124,* 1–9. doi: 10.1542/peds.2009-1522

Lord, C., & McGee, J. P. (Eds.). (2001). *Educating children with autism.* Washington, DC: National Academy Press. Available from http://www.nap.edu/catalog.php?record_id = 10017

Rice, C. E., Baio, J., Van Naarden Braun, K., Doernberg, N., Meaney, F. J., & Kirby, R. S. (2007). A public health collaboration for the surveillance of autism spectrum disorders. *Paediatric and Perinatal Epidemiology, 21,* 179–190. doi: 10.1111/j .1365-3016.2007.00801.x

Schopler, E., & Reichler, R. J. (1971). Developmental therapy by parents with their own autistic child. In M. Rutter (Ed.), *Infantile autism: Concepts, characteristics, and treatment* (pp. 206–227). London, United Kingdom: Churchill-Livingston.

Wieder, S., & Greenspan, S. (2001). The DIR (developmental, individual-difference, relationship-based) approach to assessment and intervention planning. Bulletin of ZERO TO THREE: *National Center for Infants, Toddlers, and Families, 21*(4), 11–19.

# 1

# Research-Based Educational Practices for Students With Autism Spectrum Disorders

*Joseph B. Ryan, Elizabeth M. Hughes, Antonis Katsiyannis, Melanie McDaniel, and Cynthia Sprinkle*

*Autism spectrum disorder (ASD) has become the fastest growing disability in the United States, with current prevalence rates estimated at as many as 1 in 110 children (CDC, 2010). This increase in the number of students identified with ASD has significant implications for public schools. The most popular research-based educational practices for teaching this population, explored in the pages that follow, include applied behavior analysis (ABA); the Developmental, Individual-Difference, Relationship-Based model (DIR/Floortime); the Picture Exchange Communication System (PECS); social stories; and Treatment and Education of Autistic and Communication related handicapped CHildren (TEACCH).*

In 1990, while amending the Education for All Handicapped Children Act, Congress expanded the number of disability categories eligible to receive special education services in public schools by including autism. Autism is a developmental disability that significantly affects an individual's verbal and nonverbal communication as well as social interaction. It is typically evident before age 3 and adversely impacts a child's educational performance. Other characteristics commonly associated with autism include: (a) engagement in repetitive activities and stereotyped movements, (b) poor eye contact, (c) difficulty socializing with others, (d) resistance to changes in daily routines, and (e) unusual responses to sensory experiences such as loud noises (Individuals With Disabilities Education Act [IDEA], 2008). Although the intelligence quotient (IQ) distribution for specific types of autism resembles that of the

1

general population, there appears to always be significant differentiation between written and oral language skills, marked emotional difficulties recognized by parents and teachers but not by the students themselves, and sensory problems similar to persons who function at a much lower cognitive level (Barnhill, Hagiwara, Myles, & Simpson, 2000). As a result, children with autism, regardless of whether they are high or low functioning, have difficulty with peer relationships and understanding social situations (Kasari, Freeman, Bauminger, & Alkin, 1999).

## AUTISTIC SPECTRUM DISORDERS

Autism is a disorder that adversely affects a child's communication, socialization, and interests prior to age 3, with the average onset at 15 months (Hutton & Caron, 2005). One aspect of *autism* that distinguishes it from other disabilities is that the term refers to a spectrum or multiple types of similarly related disorders. Hence, the disability is more commonly referred to as *autism spectrum disorder* (ASD), with symptoms ranging from mild cognitive, social, and behavioral deficits to more severe symptoms in which children may suffer from intellectual disabilities and be nonverbal. There are five subtypes of ASD.

### Autistic Disorder

Approximately one third (35%–40%) of children with autism are nonverbal (Mesibov, Adams, & Klinger, 1997). The majority of students diagnosed with autism have IQ scores categorizing them with intellectual disability, with only one third (25%–33%) having an IQ in the average or above-average range (Heflin & Alaimo, 2007).

### Asperger's Syndrome

Individuals with Asperger's syndrome typically do not exhibit delays in the area of verbal communication, and often develop large vocabularies. However, they do show impairments in their ability to understand nonverbal communication or the pragmatics of language. As a result, even though many individuals may be very high functioning cognitively (e.g., Temple Grandin, an internationally renowned author) they often experience significant social skill deficits.

### Childhood Disintegrative Disorder (CDD)

CDD is a very rare disorder (1/50,000) that typically affects males. It is characterized by a period of normal development followed by an onset of autism-related symptoms, including marked losses of motor, language, and social skills. Symptoms may appear as early as age 2, although most develop the symptoms between 3 and 4 years of age (National Institute of Mental Health, 2008).

## Rett Syndrome

In contrast to CDD, Rett's is a rare genetic disorder (1/15,000) that almost exclusively affects females. The disorder is characterized by a period of normal development followed by a deceleration of head growth accompanied by an increase in autism-related symptoms (between 6 and 18 months). Other symptoms include regression in mental and social development, loss of language, seizures, and loss of hand skills that results in a constant hand-wringing motion (Heward, 2009).

## Pervasive Developmental Disorder Not Otherwise Specified (PDD-NOS)

PDD-NOS is most commonly used to describe children who exhibit at least one characteristic of an ASD subtype, but do not meet all of the specific diagnostic criteria (American Psychiatric Association, 2000). As a result, children who suffer from a qualitative difference from their peers in communication, socialization, or interests and activities may receive a diagnosis of PDD-NOS.

## INCREASE IN PREVALENCE RATES OF ASD

Perhaps the most alarming aspect of ASD for school systems has been the dramatic and continued increase in prevalence rates of ASD across the United States over the past 2 decades. When a new disability first becomes eligible for special education services, it is often anticipated prevalence rates will rise as school systems begin to actively screen children for the disability. This increase in numbers of children served should be expected within the first several years, as was seen with the increased prevalence of traumatic brain injury (TBI), which was added as a disability category the same year as autism. However, after 2 years, the growth rate for children identified with TBI began to plateau, while the prevalence rate for children with ASD has continued to grow nearly 2 decades later (Newschaffer, Falb, & Gurney, 2005).

In 1992, the year following ASD eligibility under IDEA, only 5,415 students with ASD were declared eligible for IDEA services (U.S. Department of Education, 1995), representing less than one percent (.1%) of all students with disabilities. A decade later the number of students receiving special education services for ASD reached 97,204 (1.66% of all students with disabilities; U.S. Department of Education, 2003) an increase of 1,708%. In comparison, the percentage increase for all disabilities during this same period was just 30.38%. By the last count, the prevalence rate has continued to increase, surpassing a quarter million students (292,818), and now accounts for 4.97% of all students with disabilities (U.S. Department of Education, 2008). This represents a dramatic increase of 201.24% since 2002, and a 5,307.53% increase since the category was first established. The Centers for Disease Control and Prevention (CDC)'s Autism and Developmental

Disabilities Monitoring Network estimated that approximately 1 in 110 children may have ASD (CDC, 2010).

## CAUSES OF AUTISM

The etiology of ASD is currently unknown. The combination of skyrocketing prevalence rates and lack of knowledge regarding the cause of ASD has sent concerned parents and educators searching for answers through both traditional (e.g., news media and professional journals) and informal (e.g., World Wide Web blogging) informational outlets. Unfortunately, this has sometimes resulted in further confusion as consumers are left to sift through a combination of research, speculation, and misinformation for answers. Given that ASD is a spectrum of disorders, it is very likely there are multiple causes (Halsey, Hyman, & the Conference Writing Panel, 2001); current research focuses on both biological and environmental factors. From a biological or genetic perspective, researchers have observed structural and chemical differences in the brain of children with ASD as early as the first trimester's development of the fetus (Halsey et al., 2001). These findings, coupled with increased prevalence rates among family members with a history of the disorder, add credence to possible genetic causes.

Related to the biological theory is the controversial view that ASD is caused by a compromised immune system resulting from exposure to vaccinations. As a result, there has been significant concern over the use of childhood vaccinations, specifically those containing thimerosal, a mercury-based preservative. The National Institutes of Health (NIH), the American Academy of Pediatrics, and several other medical organizations stress there is no research to support this link (Halsey et al., 2001). Medical professionals emphasize that most vaccinations developed after 2001 no longer contain thimerosal, and caution that the increasing trend of parental refusal to vaccinate their children has resulted in increased outbreaks of the potentially fatal childhood diseases these vaccinations were designed to prevent. Still, there is a continued call for research to further explore if certain children are more susceptible to developing degenerating types of ASD after being administered vaccinations, especially because the age at which many vaccinations are administered correlates with the onset of the degenerative forms of ASD.

Although there is also concern that ASD may result from environmental toxins, there has been no empirical research to support this claim. Heflin and Alaimo (2007) cautioned that although it has been observed that specific geographical areas have been shown to contain higher concentrations of ASD, this may be the result of families either (a) moving to areas that provide better educational services for their children with ASD, or (b) these locales are more effective at screening and identifying the disorder.

## IMPLICATIONS FOR SCHOOLS

The continued increase of students identified with ASD has placed significant stressors on public schools and the educators that serve them. Points of contention between parents and school districts include (a) eligibility and services provided, (b) educational placement (e.g., least-restrictive environment), and (c) instructional methodologies (Yell, Katsiyannis, Drasgow, & Herbst, 2003; Zirkel, 2002).

In respect to eligibility and services, Yell and Drasgow (2000, p. 213) recommended that (a) school districts ensure timely eligibility decisions based on evaluations by professionals with experience in ASD, (b) educators develop individualized education programs (IEPs) that address all the areas of need identified in the evaluation, and (c) services identified in the IEP result in meaningful educational benefit to the student (e.g., districts must monitor student progress toward IEP goals and objectives). In accordance with federal law, districts must place students with disabilities in integrated settings to the maximum extent appropriate and adopt empirically validated instructional strategies and programs. In addition, using empirically validated methodologies is particularly important given the emphasis of the No Child Left Behind Act of 2001 on incorporating evidence-based methodologies and related provisions in IDEA regarding services outlined in a student's IEP (see Simpson, 2005). Specifically, IEPs require "a statement of the special education and related services and supplementary aids and services, based on peer-reviewed research to the extent practicable" (IDEA, 20 U.S.C. & 1414[d][1][A][i][IV]).

Unfortunately, given the number of non-evidence-based interventions currently marketed for the treatment of ASD (e.g., facilitated communication, holding therapy, secretin therapy), selecting efficacious interventions can be a challenging proposition for both the lay and professional consumer alike. Table 1 summarizes the most popular research-based educational practices for teaching students with ASD, a good starting point for educators seeking effective interventions.

## EVIDENCE-BASED EDUCATIONAL PROGRAMS FOR STUDENTS WITH ASD

### Applied Behavior Analysis (Lovaas/Discrete Trial Training)

In 1957, noted behaviorist B. F. Skinner extended the concept of operant conditioning and rewarding positive behaviors to verbal behavior—meaning behavior is under the control of consequences mediated by other people. Skinner's research shaped the way researchers and educators alike looked at behavior. His research became a catalyst for further investigation into how theories of behavior, referred to as *applied behavior analysis* (ABA), could be

**Table 1. Evidence-Based Interventions for Students With Autism Spectrum Disorders**

| Intervention | Program Description | Demonstrated Efficacy | Internet Link |
|---|---|---|---|
| Developmental, Individual-Difference, Relationship-Based Model (DIR/Floortime; Wieder & Greenspan, 2001) | Through challenging yet child-friendly play experiences, clinicians, parents, and educators learn about the strengths and limitations of the child, therefore gaining the ability to tailor interventions as necessary while strengthening the bond between the parent and child and fostering social and emotional development of the child. *Time requirement:* 14–35 hours per week | Increased levels of: • Social functioning • Emotional functioning • Information gathering *For ages:* Approximately 2–5 years | www.icdl.com This Interdisciplinary Council on Developmental and Learning Disorders site allows professionals to learn more about the DIR/Floortime model, DIR institutions and workshops, and current research regarding DIR/Floortime. |
| Discrete Trial Training (DTT; Lovaas, 1987) | Intervention that focuses on managing a child's learning opportunities by teaching specific, manageable tasks until mastery in a continued effort to build upon the mastered skills. *Time requirement:* 20–30 hours per week across settings | Increased levels of: • Cognitive skills • Language skills • Adaptive skills • Compliance skills *For ages:* Approximately 2–6 years | www.helpingtogrow. istores.com www.aba. insightcommerce.net www.adaptivechild.com These commercial sites provide opportunities to purchase programs and adaptive equipment. |
| Lovaas Method (Lovaas, 1987) | Intervention that focuses on managing a child's learning opportunities by teaching specific, manageable tasks until mastery in a continued effort to build upon the mastered skills. *Time requirement:* 20–40 hours per week | Increased levels of: • Adaptive skills • Cognitive skills • Compliance skills • Language skills • IQ • Social functioning *For ages:* Approximately 2–12 years | www.lovaas.com Official site for Lovaas Institute that provides detailed information about Lovaas method, success stories, services, and products available. |

*continues*

**Table 1.** *Continued*

| Intervention | Program Description | Demonstrated Efficacy | Internet Link |
|---|---|---|---|
| Picture Exchange Communication System (PECS; Bondy & Frost, 1994) | Communication system developed to assist students in building fundamental language skills, eventually leading to spontaneous communication. The tiered intervention supports the learner in learning to identify, discriminate between, and then exchange different symbols with a partner as a means to communicate a want. *Time requirement:* As long as the child is engaged, typically 20–30 minutes per session | Increased levels of: <br> • Speech and language development <br> • Social-communicative behaviors <br> *For ages:* Approximately 2 years–adult | www.PECS.com <br> Official site; provides information regarding PECS training courses, consultation, certification, and products. |
| Social stories (Gray & Garand, 1993) | Personalized stories that systematically describe a situation, skill, or concept in terms of relevant social cues, perspectives, and common responses, modeling and providing a socially accepted behavior option. *Time requirement:* Time requirements vary per story; approximately 5–10 min prior to difficult situation | Increased levels of: <br> • Prosocial behaviors <br> *For ages:* Approximately 2–12 years | www.thegraycenter.org <br> This site provides information about resources available through the Center, including products on how to make and use social stories. The site also provides general information about autism and research that supports the use of social stories. |
| Treatment and Education of Autistic and Communication related handicapped CHildren (TEACCH; Schopler & Reichler, 1971) | Intervention that supports task completion by providing explicit instruction and visual supports in a purposefully structured environment, planned to meet the unique task needs of the student. *Time requirement:* Up to 25 hours per week (during the school day) | Increased levels of: <br> • Imitation <br> • Perception <br> • Gross motor skills <br> • Hand–eye coordination <br> • Cognitive performance <br> *For ages:* Approximately 6 years–adult | www.teacch.com <br> The site is operated through a division of the University of North Carolina Department of Psychology and provides links to regional centers, programs and services, as well as access to current research and publications supporting the method. |

used within educational settings. Generally speaking, ABA is a systematic process of studying and modifying observable behavior through a manipulation of the environment (Chiesa, 2004). The theory characterizes the components of any behavior by an A-B-C model: the antecedent to the behavior (A; stimulus/event that occurs prior to the behavior), the behavior itself (B; child's action in response to a stimulus), and the consequence (C; outcome or result of the behavior). In recent years, the principles of this theory of behavior have been used to create a behavior modification program sharing the same name, designed for the treatment of individuals with cognitive and behavioral deficits, including ASD.

Clinical psychologist Ivar Lovaas first provided evidence of the effectiveness of ABA programs for children with ASD. In this seminal study (Lovaas, 1987), one group of children less than 4 years old received an intensive treatment of ABA called discrete trial training (DTT) over a span of 2 to 3 years. DTT is an instructional strategy in which a specific task (also called a trial) is isolated and taught by being repeatedly presented to the student. Responses are recorded for each command and the trial is continued until the student demonstrates mastery of the task. Specifically, DTT consists of (a) presenting a discriminative stimulus to the student (e.g., teacher asks student what sound the letter $p$ makes), (b) occurrence or approximation of target response from the student (e.g., student attempts to make the $p$ sound), (c) delivery of reinforcing consequence (e.g., teacher claps hands and smiles replying with the proper sound of the letter $p$), and (d) specified intertrial interval (e.g., teacher repeats request after specific lapsed time).

In order to promote success, ABA programs require consistent, intense, sometimes almost constant feedback and correction of a child's behavior. Therefore, intense one-on-one instruction is recommended at the beginning of the intervention (e.g., 20–30 hours per week), and parent participation is crucial to help ensure learned behaviors generalize across environments (e.g., home and school). As the new behavior replaces the old behavior and becomes more automatic, the parent or teacher implementing the intervention must methodically lessen interaction and feedback with the child during the targeted behavior.

Lovaas (1987) reported that nearly half (47%) of the children in the ABA program achieved higher functioning in comparison to only 2% of the control group not receiving treatment. Though this particular study was criticized for questionable research practices, it has since been replicated with similar results (Cohen, Amerine-Dickins, & Smith, 2006; Howard, Sparkman, Cohen, Green, & Sanislaw, 2005). This body of research includes several studies which reported half (50%) of the children with ASD treated with ABA prior to age 4 showed significant increases in IQ, verbal ability, and/or social functioning (Lovaas, 1987). Even those who did not show dramatic improvements had significantly better improvement than matched children in the control groups. In addition, some children who received ABA therapy were eventually able to attend classes with their nondisabled peers. This research suggests intensive ABA interventions implemented early in a child's development can result in long-term positive outcomes. ABA and DTT have an extensive body of research that supports its use in academic and behavior interventions for children with ASD (Simpson, 2004) as well as other intellectual disabilities (Iwata et al., 1997), and are considered to be scientifically based practices for treating individuals with ASD (Simpson, 2005).

## Developmental, Individual-Difference, Relationship-Based Approach Model/Floortime

The Developmental, Individual Differences, Relationship-Based model (DIR; Wieder & Greenspan, 2001) is a comprehensive, interdisciplinary approach to treating children with disabilities, specifically those with ASD. It focuses on the child's individual developmental needs, including social-emotional functioning, communication skills, thinking and learning processes, motor skills, body awareness, and attention span. The DIR model serves as a framework to understand the developmental profile of an infant or child and the family by developing relationships and interactions between the child and parent. It enables caregivers, educators, and clinicians to plan an assessment and intervention program that is tailored to the specific needs of the child and their family. It is not necessarily an intervention, but rather a method of analysis and understanding that helps organize the many intervention components into a comprehensive program (Wieder & Greenspan, 2001).

A vital element of the DIR model is Floortime (Wieder & Greenspan, 2001). Floortime serves both as an intervention and as a philosophy for interacting with children. It aims to create opportunities for children to experience the critical developmental stages they are lacking through intensive play experiences. It can be implemented as a procedure within the home, school, or as a part of a child's different therapies. A Floortime program initially involves one-on-one experiences between the parent or caregiver and the child. These experiences are typically 20- to 30-minute periods when parents literally get on the floor with their children and interact and play in a way that challenges typical behaviors (e.g., repetitive movements, isolation, inappropriate play) and encourages appropriate, interactive play and socialization through parent-directed modeling and prompting.

This intervention aims to train parents and teachers to engage the emotions of even the most withdrawn toddler by entering the child's world. School systems sometimes incorporate aspects of this model into their programs but generally do not make this their primary means of educating young children with ASD. Controlled research supporting Floortime is limited, but supports a positive outcome for children with ASD. A pilot study using the PLAY Project Home Consultation program (see http://www.playproject. org/), a training program for parents of young children with ASD incorporating Floortime (Wieder & Greenspan, 2001), found that nearly half (45.5%) of the children made significant functional developmental progress through the program and reported a 90% approval rating from parents involved in the program (Solomon, Necheles, Ferch, & Bruckman, 2007).

With its strong emphasis on social and emotional development, the Floortime model (Wieder & Greenspan, 2001) may be a natural complement to a behavioral teaching program. Further research is needed promoting Floortime, but it is currently being used successfully by families who prefer a play-based therapy as a primary or secondary treatment, especially for toddlers and preschoolers (Wieder & Greenspan, 2001).

## Picture Exchange Communication System

Typical learners are constantly communicating needs, wants, and desires through socially acceptable verbal expressions and physical gestures that may not come naturally to individuals with ASD. An increasingly common intervention used to enhance communication skills of children with ASD is the Picture Exchange Communication System (PECS; Bondy & Frost, 1994). PECS is a multitiered program that promotes communication through the exchange of tactile symbols and objects. Symbols may include photographs, drawings, pictures of objects, or objects that a child is taught to associate with a desirable toy, person, or activity.

The three instructional phases of PECS teach a child to (a) request an item or activity by giving a corresponding picture, symbol, or object to his/her partner, (b) generalize the activity by bringing the request symbol to the partner who may be located in different areas of the room, and (c) discriminate between two different request symbols before bringing it to the partner (Lund & Troha, 2008). The six-phase PECS program extends beyond discrimination of two symbols to the discrimination of many symbols and incorporates more complex language exchange between interventionist and student (Bondy & Frost, 1994).

PECS (Bondy & Frost, 1994) requires the instructor to teach the child to request a desired activity through modeling (i.e., demonstration of desired behavior). The child is prompted by the teacher to use the tactile symbols to make a specific request (e.g., student points to picture of glass of water to express desire for a drink). It is important to create symbols that are significant and personal to the child, which will accurately communicate what the child is requesting. The child is positively reinforced for correctly using the appropriate symbols and essentially associates the symbol with a desired activity. This in turn increases the probability the child will continue to use the symbol to request that specific activity (e.g., water break) in the future. It is equally important that the child is corrected whenever the symbols are used incorrectly (e.g., the child screams for drink), therefore decreasing the chances that an inappropriate method of communication will be repeated.

The various tiers of PECS (Bondy & Frost, 1994) gradually increase in complexity as tasks become more difficult. Although verbal and gestural prompting (e.g., pointing) may be necessary at the beginning of each phase, it should be faded as the student demonstrates mastery of the skill (e.g., teacher refrains from asking the child which picture will ask for water once the child consistently uses the object correctly). Teaching the child to generalize the behavior learned is critical for the behavior to be functional and applicable to daily life. Behavior generalization is naturally incorporated into PECS during the second stage when the partner physically moves farther away from the child, and during the third stage when the child is taught to discriminate between different symbols (e.g., glass of water and glass of milk).

Research supports PECS (Bondy & Frost, 1994) as a promising practice for teaching individuals with ASD how to more appropriately communicate requests (Carr & Felce, 2006; Ganz & Simpson, 2004; Simpson, 2005). Due in part to the prescribed order of teaching, PECS may be very beneficial for individuals who are either nonverbal or have limited communication skills. Lund and Troha (2008) also provided preliminary evidence that a modified version of PECS using objects as symbols in the place of pictures may be used successfully to facilitate communication skills for children who have the comorbid condition of ASD and blindness.

## Social Stories

Social stories (Gray & Garand, 1993) provide a brief descriptive story for children to help them better understand specific social situations. Social stories describe "a situation, skill, or concept in terms of relevant social cues, perspectives, and common responses in a specifically defined style and format" (The Gray Center for Social Learning and Understanding, n.d.). The goal of social stories is not to change an individual's behavior but rather to expose the individual to a better understanding of an event, thereby encouraging an alternative and proper response. Less formally, the teacher and student may create personalized stories that explicitly inform the child what to expect in a given situation that has proven to be difficult in the past (e.g., riding the school bus, participating in an assembly), and in turn how the child should act in the particular situation. Social stories can be used either to encourage replacement of a child's maladaptive behaviors (e.g., screaming to get a teacher's attention) or to promote prosocial behaviors (e.g., introducing yourself to person entering a room; Spencer, Simpson, & Lynch, 2008).

Social stories are typically presented to the child before the situation occurs as a way to help rehearse the scenario. For example, if a child has difficulty riding the school bus, the teacher and student could develop a social story regarding how the student should board and ride the bus, and why that behavior is necessary. The story should also include positive behaviors that the child does well, other events that may serve as behavioral triggers (e.g., other children violating student's personal space), and how the individual could best respond to each situation (Sansosti, Powell-Smith, & Kincaid, 2004; Scattone, Wilczynski, Edwards, & Rabian, 2002). In addition to reading the story, the child may require prompting during social situations, and may need to practice the skill presented in the story. Recognition of appropriate behavior by the student is vital, reinforcing appropriate behaviors with an ultimate goal of self-regulation and management (Spencer et al., 2008).

Social stories should be written and illustrated at a level in keeping with the cognitive ability of the student they serve. Gray developed clear guidelines (see The Gray Center for Social Learning and Understanding, n.d.) for developing a story, which typically ranges from 5 to 10 sentences. Stories should: (a) define a specific target behavior of concern, (b) identify an appropriate replacement behavior, (c) be written from the child's perspective, (d) include pictures or drawings to help the child relate to the desired behavior, and (e) include a ratio of one directive sentence for every two to five sentences that are either descriptive, perspective, or both.

Specifically, directive sentences define the goal of the story and provide responses or behaviors the student is expected to perform. *Descriptive* sentences provide details regarding the event, setting, thoughts, or actions of people in a similar situation. *Perspective* sentences are usually related to consequences or outcomes of the situation and describe how other people may react or feel based on the action or inaction of the main character of the story. Additionally, stories may include *affirmative* sentences that provide statements of social value (Ali & Frederickson, 2006; Sansosti et al., 2004), *control* sentences that reinforce the student's method of self-regulation and affirm the right to choose, and *cooperative* sentences that provide names of responsive people who may assist in the student's efforts or may be impacted by their choices. Some of the sentences may also have blanks for the student to fill in (Ali & Frederickson, 2006). As with any good story, a title, introduction, body, and conclusion are important elements (Quilty, 2007). The format of the social story should be predictable. It should not merely be a list of tasks, but should describe behaviors rather than simply directing the child.

Although the research is not yet extensive, the use of social stories is considered a promising behavioral intervention for children with ASD (Simpson, 2005), helping to increase desirable prosocial behaviors such as hand washing, delayed echolalia, following directions, and using a quiet voice (as reviewed by Sansosti et al., 2004); and to decrease undesirable, maladaptive behaviors such as calling out in class (Crozier & Tincani, 2005), hitting, screaming, falling from a chair, and crying while completing homework (Adams, Gouvousis, VanLue, & Waldron, 2004). Although full confirmation supporting the efficacy of social stories for children with ASD is premature until larger scale research studies are conducted, early findings appear to be very promising.

## Treatment and Education of Autistic and Communication Related Handicapped CHildren (TEACCH)

The TEACCH program has been used to educate children with ASD for over 3 decades. Based on Eric Schopler's work in the 1970s (e.g., Schopler & Reichler, 1971), TEACCH uses structured teaching, which highlights the use of visual supports, to maximize the independent functioning of a child with ASD and/or other related disorders (Hume & Odem, 2007). TEACCH is composed of four critical, structured teaching components: (a) physical structure and organization of the work space, (b) schedules indicating details about the required task, (c) work systems depicting detailed expectations of the individual during the task, and (d) task organization explicitly describing the learning task. The TEACCH system requires the environment to be arranged to meet the unique needs of the child in a given situation. For example, if a child is expected to perform specific homework tasks, the TEACCH program requires the desk area at home be set up in a way that prompts the child to self-monitor personal behavior while working through the tasks necessary to complete the homework assignment (e.g., take out homework, put name on page, read directions, ask for assistance, put completed homework in folder, place folder in book bag). TEACCH may also be used with older students to help prepare them for the workplace by maximizing task independence. For example, a worker whose task it is to sort and stack different materials can use TEACCH to remain on task and efficiently perform the responsibilities required with minimum supervision.

TEACCH requires that the child receive explicit instruction on how to maximize the use of the physical work space through either physical or visual prompts. The adult supervisor may model how the organized space is used to cue different performance steps and monitor the individual as these tasks are being mastered. Primary reinforces are frequently used to increase desired behavior (e.g., verbal praise, recognition, time for desired activity). Staff should prompt and reward the student as necessary, decreasing prompts as the student becomes more self-sufficient and requires less adult supervision.

Although there have been no large-scale studies to date investigating TEACCH, it has been found to be a promising intervention for students with ASD (Simpson, 2005). Studies have demonstrated increases in fine and gross motor skills, functional independence, on-task behavior, play behavior, imitation behavior, and other functional living skills, while reducing the need for teacher prompts (Hume & Odom, 2007; Tsang, Shek, Lam, Tang, & Cheung, 2007). TEACCH has demonstrated efficacy for children with ASD across various ages and ability levels.

## FINAL THOUGHTS

Identifying effective interventions to use with children who have ASD can be challenging for educators and parents alike, especially when various fads and "quick-fix" solutions may receive as much if not more press than evidence-based approaches. The current emphasis on implementing evidence-based interventions leads educators and parents to seek out programs supported by data from empirical research. Although there is a growing body of quality research available on effective interventions for children with ASD, it is still fairly limited, especially given the increasing prevalence rates and wide range of educational, verbal, and social skill deficits associated with this disability.

# REFERENCES

Adams, L., Gouvousis, A., VanLue, M., & Waldron, C. (2004). Social story interventions: Improving communication skills in a child with autism spectrum disorder. *Focus on Autism and Other Developmental Disorders, 19,* 87–94.

Ali, S., & Frederickson, N. (2006). Investigating the evidence base of social stories. *Educational Psychology in Practice, 22,* 355–377.

American Psychiatric Association. (2000). *Diagnostic and statistical manual of mental disorders* (3rd ed. text rev.). Arlington, VA: Author.

Barnhill, G., Hagiwara, T., Myles, B. S., & Simpson, R. L. (2000). Asperger syndrome: A study of the cognitive profiles of 37 children and adolescents. *Focus on Autism and Other Disabilities, 15,* 146–153.

Bondy, A., & Frost, L. (1994). The picture exchange communication system. *Focus on Autistic Behavior, 9*(3), 1–19.

Carr, D., & Felce, J. (2006). Brief report: Increase in production of spoken words in some children with autism after PECS teaching to Phase III. *Journal of Autism and Developmental Disorders, 37,* 780–787.

Centers for Disease Control and Prevention. (2010, November). Prevalence of autism spectrum disorders. *MMWR Surveillance Summaries, 56*(SS-1), 1–28. Retrieved from http://www.cdc.gov/mmwr/indss_2007.html

Chiesa, M. (2004). *Radical behaviorism: The philosophy & the science.* Boston, MA: Authors Cooperative.

Cohen, H., Amerine-Dickins M., & Smith, T. (2006). Early intensive behavioral treatment: Replication of the UCLA model in a community setting. *Journal of Developmental & Behavioral Pediatrics, 27,* 145–155.

Crozier, S., & Tincani, M. (2005). Using a modified social story to decrease disruptive behavior of a child with autism. *Focus on Autism and Other Developmental Disabilities, 20,* 150–157.

Ganz, J., & Simpson, R. (2004). Effects on communicative requesting and speech development of the picture exchange communication system in children with characteristics of autism. *Journal of Autism and Developmental Disorders, 34,* 395–409.

Gray, C. A., & Garand, J. D. (1993). Social stories. Improving responses of students with autism with accurate social information. *Focus on Autistic Behavior, 8,* 1–10.

The Gray Center for Social Learning and Understanding. (n.d.). *What are social stories?* Zeeland, MI: Author. Retrieved from http://www.thegraycenter.org/social-stories/what-are-social-stories

Halsey N., Hyman S., & the Conference Writing Panel. (2001). Measles-mumps-rubella vaccine and autistic spectrum disorders. *Pediatrics, 107*(5), 84–107

Heflin, J. L., & Alaimo, D. F. (2007). *Students with autism spectrum disorder.* Upper Saddle River, NJ: Pearson/Merrill Prentice Hall.

Heward, W. L. (2009). *Exceptional children: An introduction to special education* (9th ed.). Upper Saddle River, NJ: Pearson/Merrill Prentice Hall.

Howard, J. S., Sparkman, C. R., Cohen, H. G., Green, G., & Sanislaw, H. A. (2005). A comparison of intensive behavior analytic and eclectic treatments for young children with autism. *Research in Developmental Disabilities, 26,* 359–383.

Hume, K., & Odom, S. (2007). Effects of an individual work system on the independent functioning of students with autism. *Journal of Autism and Developmental Disorders, 37,* 1166–1180.

Hutton, A. M., & Caron, S. L. (2005). Experience of families and children with autism in rural New England. *Focus on Autism and Other Developmental Disabilities, 20,* 180–190.

Individuals With Disabilities Education Act of 2004, 20 U.S.C. §§ 1414 *et seq.* (2008).

Iwata, B., Bailey, J., Neef, N., Wacker, D., Repp, A., & Shook, G. (Eds.). (1997). *Behavior analysis in developmental disabilities (1968-1995).* Bloomington, IN: Society for the Experimental Analysis of Behavior.

Kasari, C., Freeman, S. F. N., Bauminger, N., & Alkin, M. C. (1999). Parental perspectives on inclusion: Effects of autism and Down syndrome. *Journal of Autism and Developmental Disorders, 29,* 297–305.

Lovaas, O. I. (1987). Behavioral treatment and normal educational and intellectual functioning in young autistic children. *Journal of Consulting and Clinical Psychology, 55,* 3–9.

Lund, S., & Troha, J. (2008). Teaching young people who are blind and have autism to make requests using a variation on the picture exchange communication system with tactile symbols: A preliminary investigation. *Journal of Autism and Development Disorders, 38,* 719–730.

Mesibov, G. B., Adams, L. W., & Klinger, L. G. (1997). *Autism: Understanding the disorder.* New York, NY: Plenum.

National Institute of Mental Health. (2008). *Autism spectrum disorders (pervasive developmental disorders).* Retrieved from http://www.nimh.nih.gov/health/publications/autism/index.shtml

Newschaffer, C. J., Flab, M. D., & Gurney, J. G. (2005). National autism prevalence trends from the United States special education data. *Pediatrics, 115,* 277–282.

Quilty, K. M. (2007) Teaching paraprofessionals how to write and implement social stories for students with autism spectrum disorders. *Remedial and Special Education, 28,* 182–189.

Sansosti, F., Powell-Smith, K., & Kincaid, D. (2004). A research synthesis of social story interventions for children with autism spectrum disorder. *Focus on Autism and Other Developmental Disorders, 19,* 194–204.

Scattone, D., Wilczynski, S. M., Edwards, R. P., & Rabian, B. (2002). Decreasing disruptive behaviors of children with autism using social stories. *Journal of Autism and Developmental Disorders, 32,* 535–542.

Schopler, E., & Reichler, R. J. (1971). Developmental therapy by parents with their own autistic child. In M. Rutter (Ed.), *Infantile autism: Concepts, characteristics, and treatment* (pp. 206–227). London, United Kingdom: Churchill-Livingston.

Simpson, R. L. (2004). Finding effective intervention and personnel preparation practices for students with autism spectrum disorder. *Exceptional Children, 70,* 135–149.

Simpson, R. L. (2005). Evidence-based practices and students with autism spectrum disorders. *Focus on Autism and Other Developmental Disabilities, 20,* 140–149.

Skinner, B. F. (1957). *Verbal behavior.* East Norwalk, CT: Appleton-Century-Crofts.

Solomon, R., Necheles, J., Ferch, C., & Bruckman, D. (2007). Pilot study of a parent training program for young children with autism: The PLAY project home consultation program. *Autism: The International Journal of Research and Practice, 11,* 205–224.

Spencer, V. G., Simpson, C. G., & Lynch, S. A. (2008). Using social stories to increase positive behaviors for children with autism spectrum disorders. *Intervention in School & Clinic, 44,* 58–61.

Tsang, S., Shek, D., Lam, L., Tang., F., & Cheung, P. (2007). Brief report: Application of the TEACCH program on Chinese pre-school children with autism—Does culture make a difference? *Journal of Autism and Developmental Disorders, 37,* 390–396.

U.S. Department of Education. (1995). *Seventeenth annual report to Congress on the implementation of the Individuals with Disabilities Education Act.* Washington, DC: Author. Retrieved from http://www2.ed.gov/pubs/OSEP95AnlRpt/index.html

U.S. Department of Education. (2003). *Twenty-fifth annual report to Congress on the implementation of the Individuals with Disabilities Education Act.* Washington, DC: Author. Retrieved from http://www.ed.gov/about/reports/annual/osep/2003/index.html

U.S. Department of Education. (2008). *Individuals with Disabilities Education Act (IDEA) data.* Retrieved from http://www.ideadata.org/PartBdata.asp

Wieder, S., & Greenspan, S. (2001). The DIR (developmental, individual-difference, relationship-based) approach to assessment and intervention planning. *Bulletin of ZERO TO THREE: National Center for Infants, Toddlers, and Families, 21*(4), 11–19.

Yell, M. L., & Drasgow, E. (2000). Litigating a free appropriate public education: The Lovaas hearings and cases. *The Journal of Special Education, 33,* 205–214.

Yell, M. L., Katsiyannis, A., Drasgow, E., & Herbst, M. (2003). Developing legally correct and educationally appropriate programs for students with autism spectrum disorders. *Focus on Autism and Other Developmental Disabilities, 18,* 182–191.

Zirkel, P. A. (2002). The autism case law: Administrative and judicial rulings. *Focus on Autism and Other Developmental Disabilities, 17,* 84–93.

Originally published in *TEACHING Exceptional Children,* Vol. 43, No. 3, pp. 56–64.

# 2

# Interventions for Increasing the Academic Engagement of Students With Autism Spectrum Disorders in Inclusive Classrooms

*Gay Goodman and Cathy M. Williams*

*Joseph, a student with autism in Ms. Mendez's inclusion kindergarten class, experienced difficulty attending during group activities. He spent a significant amount of time looking at his hands and quoting parts of his favorite videos. Attempts to engage Joseph resulted in vocal protests and, at times, mild aggression. Ms. Mendez realized that she needed to address those behaviors but was unsure of how to do so. She consulted with an Intervention Assistance Team (IAT) whose members had experience designing appropriate interventions for the problem behaviors of students with autism. They generated a number of hands-on activities to help Joseph maintain his visual engagement during the group learning activity. This article describes empirically supported, field-tested strategies that have resulted in increased engagement and fewer problem behaviors for Joseph and other students with autism spectrum disorders (ASD) who are being educated in inclusive classrooms.*

Recent legislation supporting the right of all students to access the general education curriculum and instructional environment, along with empirical support attesting to the efficacy of inclusive education (see box, "What Does the Literature Say?"), has redefined the roles of special education teachers, general education teachers, paraprofessionals, and other service providers whose expertise is required for teaching students with disabilities in inclusive educational venues. Many students with disabilities are now included in general education classes for a majority of the school day. Their success in that environment often depends on the collective expertise of educational professionals working together to assist the student in attaining prosocial and proacademic goals. This statement is certainly true for students with ASD, many of whom are now instructed exclusively in general education classes.

The increased numbers of students with ASD that educators encounter in mainstream settings result not only from legal and empirical support for this placement option but also from increases in the incidence of this disorder. The Centers for Disease Control and Prevention (2006) reported that the occurrence of autism has increased from 2 to 6 children per 1000. Between 1994 and 2003, the number of students receiving special education services with an autism diagnosis increased six-fold. Even those figures may be underestimated, because not all children with ASD receive special education services under that label.

Students diagnosed with ASD often present unique and challenging behaviors that impede their success in inclusive classrooms. For example, they may demonstrate perseverative and self-stimulatory behaviors, impairments in social interactions and relationships, and impaired communication and language skills. As a result, they often display a limited range of interests, lack peer relationships, and resist participation in games and activities (American Psychiatric Association [APA], 2000), all of which are contrary to common characteristics for same-grade peers in general education settings. Those deficits can jeopardize student learning, not only because they interfere with relationships but also because they interfere with the learning envi-

## What Does the Literature Say About Including Students With ASD?

Despite ongoing debate, the inclusion of students with ASD in general education classes continues to be a recommended practice. It is, first of all, considered a civil right that has been supported by legislation since Public Law 94-142 was passed in 1975. This landmark legislation along with other legislation passed soon after made discrimination against persons on the basis of the presence of a disability illegal. Additionally, persons with disabilities are guaranteed a free and appropriate education in the least restrictive environment. The 1990 amendment (IDEA) to this law increased the protection of student rights by adding that every child should receive a free and appropriate education that is individualized to meet specific needs (Schreibman, 2005). More recently, the 2004 amendments to IDEA continue to support inclusion for students with disabilities in the least restrictive environment that is appropriate for the student.

Another reason inclusion receives continued support is that it has been found to result in gains in social development (Schreibman, 2005). Learning to function with various types of people in more complex group settings offers important benefits for students with disabilities. When placed in restrictive settings, students with ASD tend to interact with instructors rather than develop peer relationships (Donnellan, Mesaros, & Anderson, 1984). Researchers have found that, when compared with those enrolled in self-contained programs, students who participated in inclusive programs improved as much or more in the area of social competence (Fisher & Meyer, 2002).

Finally, support for inclusion is based on reports of positive academic outcomes. Although results of studies have been mixed (Harrower & Dunlap, 2001), evidence has suggested that inclusion increases academic gains, particularly for those who demonstrate greater intellectual abilities (Schreibman, 2005).

ronment for students with ASD as well as for others. In addition, the behavior exhibited by students with ASD may be interpreted as noncompliant or even defiant (Marks et al., 2003).

Because of the deficits that are characteristic of students with ASD, general education teachers, as well as special education teachers, who are preparing these students for inclusion must be well equipped with the most effective instructional strategies available, as based on documented evidence (Harrower & Dunlap, 2001). If not, deficit behaviors are likely to interfere with the successful inclusion of students with ASD in general education classrooms.

The professional literature does provide teachers with information based on research findings. Rogers (2000), however, noted that strategies researched in well-controlled laboratory settings may be difficult for classroom teachers to implement. Some authors, therefore, have suggested that educators be provided more detailed information regarding effective interventions for students with ASD that are not only evidence-based but also field-tested—ones that are, therefore, effective and practical for use in applied settings (Marks et al., 2003).

This article provides empirically supported, evidence-based intervention strategies that have also been field-tested and found effective for improving academic and social skills in early childhood and early elementary age students with ASD who are being educated in inclusive settings. Reviewing the professional literature and constructing a repertoire of strategies that are either based on, or adapted from, empirical studies that substantiate their effectiveness in remedying social and academic skills deficits of students with ASD initially derived these interventions. Each strategy in the repertoire was categorized for its effectiveness in increasing auditory, visual, social, or physical engagement, the four main areas in which many of the behavioral characteristics and skills deficits associated with ASD can be classified (APA, 2000). Then, when a student with ASD exhibited difficulty engaging in inclusive instructional activities, the IAT, co-teacher, or general education teacher responsible for the student's education referred to the repertoire of strategies and designed an intervention that was individually tailored to the student's skills deficits and the demands of the task at hand. Finally, the interventions field-tested and found effective in these applied, elementary and early childhood settings were selected as the basis for current recommendations.

An important point to note is that each of the recommended interventions can be modified and tailored to a student's unique engagement difficulties and linked with baseline assessment data. They are, therefore, compatible with Curriculum-Based Measurement (CBM; Shapiro, 2004) and other evidence-based assessment methods suitable for documenting a student's response to intervention (RTI). Finally, each strategy has the potential of being adapted to a single-subject research design based on Differential Reinforcement of an Incompatible (DRI) behavior as the treatment variable (Alberto & Troutman, 2003, chap. 8). Strategies, therefore, have the advantage of reducing inappropriate behavior by increasing the engagement of the student in proacademic and prosocial behavior. This feature is important to the success of these strategies, because inappropriate behaviors have been shown to decrease when on-task behaviors increase (Watanabe & Sturmey, 2003).

## AUDITORY ENGAGEMENT

Students demonstrate auditory engagement by following verbal instructions and responding to questions from both teachers and peers regarding the task at hand. However, communication impairments characteristic of individuals with autism include difficulty comprehending language (APA, 2000). Many students with ASD are unable to efficiently process auditory input and may

*Social Engagement—Preferred Activity*

miss verbal cues or withdraw during verbal instruction. Teachers of students with ASD often observe that they have difficulty listening to and following directions, especially during large-group, inclusive activities. In that situation, auditory focus cues, such as ringing a bell or rhythmic clapping, that cue the whole group to become silent can be given to gain students' attention before instruction is delivered. Additionally, music has been found to help individuals with autism attain both behavioral and communication objectives (Kaplan & Steele, 2005). Therefore, during more challenging instructional events, such as transitions and extended listening activities, some children with ASD are more engaged if language is presented in song (Grandin, 2002).

## Using Songs to Facilitate Transitions

When teachers transition from one activity to another, the likelihood of misbehavior increases (Kounin, 1977). Such transition times can be especially difficult for students with autism, as they require shifts in attention and behavior. A song indicating that it is time for a change in activity may help gain students' attention by cueing the required behaviors. By selecting songs for common transitions, students learn what transition is occurring, where they are to go, and what they are to do. The song must consistently be associated with the same transition for the strategy to be effective during the acquisition phase of learning to comply with transition requests. Teachers can measure the effectiveness of this strategy by documenting the level of prompting needed or the length of time required by the students to complete the transition.

> *Example:* Judy, a 7-year-old first-grade student with autism, was easily distracted when the class was directed to put away materials. Although she initiated clean up, she soon began to perseverate on the items. Her behavior was noticed and reported by disapproving classmates, but when the teacher attempted to verbally redirect her behavior, Judy resisted and sometimes became disruptive. The teacher solved the problem by teaching the class the familiar children's song, "Clean Up, Clean Up, Everybody, Everywhere." Initially, a classroom aide provided physical prompts requiring Judy to put away toys to the rhythm of the song. As the prompts were faded, the song was a sufficient reminder of what she should be doing, and she was able to stay on task.

## Using Songs During Listening Activities

To be successfully included in general education classes, students with ASD must be able to participate in group activities, such as circle time and story time. These activities require higher level listening skills that are difficult for some students with ASD and may result in inattention and self-stimulatory behavior. To maintain engagement throughout such activities, one helpful tactic is to intersperse brief songs within verbal instruction, especially when the student with ASD seems to be "drifting" off task.

> *Example:* Jose, a 5-year-old kindergarten student, was more interested in quoting his favorite movies than attending to circle activities. Knowing that he enjoys music, his teacher began singing the days of the week before the opening activities and discussion of the calendar. She continued this approach throughout circle time, using songs to introduce the next topic. She monitored Jose's attention level by noting the frequency and duration of eye contact and his ability to respond appropriately to topic-related questions, then inserted songs as needed to maintain the group's focus.

## VISUAL ENGAGEMENT

Typically, students demonstrate visual engagement by looking at instructors or social partners, as well as the materials being presented and discussed. Students with autism, however, may become fixated on the movement of objects in the classroom and may also attend to other inappropriate visual stimuli (APA, 2000). This tendency is problematic because visual engagement is a necessary requisite for increasing social and academic independence,

*Visual Engagement—Calendar Book*

maintaining focus on salient information required for academic skill mastery, and observing age-appropriate social skills. Visual engagement is especially difficult in larger inclusive classrooms owing to the complexity of the environment. The inability of students with ASD to stay appropriately engaged often interferes with their acquisition of essential social skills and academic behaviors. The use of visual aids has been recommended to elicit a higher level of appropriate social and academic behavior on a variety of tasks in both experimental and natural learning environments (Quill, 1995), and they are equally adaptable and effective for use in applied educational settings.

## Increasing Independence

The inability of students with autism to function independently is often evident in their lack of age-appropriate, goal-directed behavior. They also exhibit little variety and creativity in the high-frequency, free-time activities they choose (Schreibman, 2005). As a result, to participate in routine classroom activities they require excessive prompting, which can be difficult for teachers to provide in inclusive classrooms. The use of visual schedules and a variety of modeling techniques can be used to increase their independence and reduce the need for continuous teacher intervention.

## Using Visual Schedules

Visual schedules are particularly helpful to students with autism because they clearly indicate what has been completed and what must be done next (Marks et al., 2003). These aids have been found to be effective in reducing the latency time between activities and in increasing students' ability to transition independently (Dettmer, Simpson, Myles, & Ganz, 2000). This strategy is easily implemented in inclusive settings, because most classroom activities are composed of component parts that can be represented visually in sequence to create schedules made up of photographs, drawings, or words (Treatment and Education of Autistic and Related Communication-handicapped Children, 2004).

*Example:* A problem tolerating the schedule existed for 6-year-old Steven who enjoyed circle time but preferred the following activity. He continuously interrupted the class by asking what was next and when circle time would be finished. The teacher tried rewarding him for speaking when given permission, but this strategy failed to decrease his interruptions. Recognizing his dependence on the teacher for schedule information, the IAT recommended a visual schedule of circle-time activities for the class. Each activity (greetings, calendar, weather, book, and song) was represented by a drawing, which, when completed, was removed from the schedule, revealing what would occur next. As Steven learned to monitor the schedule, he could see progress toward a preferred activity and was able to attend without interrupting.

Visual schedules can also be implemented during less structured activities, such as "centers." In that environment, words, symbolic picture icons, or digital photographs can be used to represent individual activities (puzzle, book, paint) or activity areas in the room (math center, library, art). A visual schedule can be created that helps students direct their own behavior throughout the work period. The effectiveness of this type of strategy is evident when the student independently directs his or her attention to the prescribed activities and as the frequency of prompting required by the student to stay on task decreases. Such schedules can be used to direct the group or to direct individual students who may be working independently on different activities at the same time. Ultimately, this strategy results in less reliance on teacher and paraprofessional assistance, an outcome that is particularly important in inclusive settings.

*Example:* Jose attended a general education kindergarten class during free centers, which included mathematics, reading, writing, art, and "dress-up." His teacher chose the centers in which he was to participate and arranged digital pictures sequentially to create a schedule. She then placed it in a location that Jose could easily access and taught him to look at the first item on the schedule and then proceed to the correct location. On completion of the first activity, Jose was taught through the use of faded prompts to remove the picture representing the completed activity and proceed to the next. This intervention resulted in his acquiring the ability to transition independently. To reinforce the use of the schedule, when he had completed it, Jose was given free time during which he chose and engaged in a highly preferred activity.

*Physical Engagement—Calendar Helper*

## Incorporating Models for Play

Children with autism tend to play with toys inappropriately or self-stimulate using parts of the toys (Schreibman, 2005). This atypical behavior interferes with their inclusion in general education classrooms because it sets them apart from their general education peers. Providing models that elicit appropriate play is, therefore, helpful. By being shown photographs of premade structures of such items as interlocking cubes, blocks, and train tracks, students who have difficulty developing and executing original ideas are provided with a model to copy. As a result, students use the materials as intended and engage in fewer stereotypical activities, as can be documented by recording the duration of time spent engaged in appropriate play.

*Example:* Isaac enjoyed building block structures; however, he tended to build the same structure several times and then lose interest in the activity. After analyzing this behavior, his special education co-teacher intervened by placing 10 digital photographs of premade block structures in the tub of blocks. Isaac was then referred to the photos and instructed to copy the structures, thus maintaining his focus in the inclusive activity for longer periods of time. As a result, he was able to engage in age-appropriate behavior and independently meet a general education academic expectation. As his skill in block building increased, the co-teacher provided increasingly complex models for Isaac.

## Maintaining Academic Group Focus

Many activities in general education, early childhood classrooms involve students' sitting as a group while attending to teachers and materials positioned in front of the class. Even though this skill is a necessary requisite for successful inclusion, it can be challenging for students with ASD, many of whom have difficulty recognizing relevant information in visually complex environments. Marks et al. (2003) recommended using "hands-on" support materials that helped students with Asperger's syndrome follow along with the information presented during instruction in general education settings. This suggestion was field-tested and found effective for students with ASD in an early childhood classroom. The students increased task completion within the required timeframe and decreased the need for redirection to task.

## Following Information Presented on Boards

Teachers' use of bulletin boards and chalkboards to display information is common practice. Such visual aids are often arranged to reflect topics discussed during circle time and other group activities. Some of the larger boards typically display such information as morning routines and spelling word lists. Children with autism may have difficulty attending to this information, as it is typically placed at a distance and in a visual field surrounded by other complex stimuli. Providing small individual replicas of the information presented on the boards for the student to hold or place on his or her desk is helpful for increasing engagement and maintaining the student's group focus.

> *Example:* Even though given preferential seating, Nathan had difficulty following along with the bulletin board materials used during circle time. His teacher, therefore, created a "hands-on" model of the bulletin board by creating miniature symbolic icons and arranging them on a laminated file folder. She then gave this folder to Nathan so that he could hold and refer to it throughout the activity. When she realized that another student was having similar difficulties, she created a book with each page representing a circle-time activity. The students initially required physical prompts to follow along, but as they demonstrated increasing independence, the paraprofessionals were able to reduce, and eventually eliminate, this assistance.

## Following Stories Read Aloud

Story time led by both teachers and peers is often part of the daily schedule for young students in general education classrooms. This activity builds important listening and language skills necessary for elementary school success. Students with ASD may have difficulty attending to the story, as they are, again, required to focus on instruction and materials from a distance. On the basis of success in their practice, Marks et al. (2003) recommended remedying this situation by providing students with their own copy of the materials, thereby enabling them to turn the pages and read along with the teacher.

> *Example:* Miss Cowley, however, found that this recommendation was not always practical in inclusive settings, for example, when two copies of reading materials are not always available. So she adapted this idea for use with Marcus, a student in her class who engaged in self-stimulatory behavior during story time. To increase his engagement, she devised simple, teacher-made books that reflected the story's main concepts and that proved to be equally effective in maintaining his group focus. The success of this intervention was evident in his increased ability to respond to questions related to the material.

## Identifying Salient Information

Children with autism tend to perseverate, having difficulty disengaging their attention and shifting from one visual stimulus to another (Landry & Bryson, 2004). In addition, they may be unable to filter excessive information and focus on main concepts and ideas. Because general education classrooms tend to be more visually complex than those that are more restrictive, this impairment may significantly interfere with students' ability to participate successfully in inclusive activities. Therefore, a recommended tactic for teachers is to highlight salient information for students with autism (Marks et al., 2003). This approach can be employed during group instruction by using materials that can be removed and presented within close visual proximity to the student.

> *Example:* Although Ms. Mendez pointed to the bulletin board to indicate what was being discussed, Joseph still had difficulty focusing on the relevant information. After consulting with the IAT, she modified the calendar bulletin board so that the days of the week and months of the year were printed on cards and attached with Velcro. Then, when discussing each topic, for example, "today," "tomorrow," and "yesterday," she removed that card from the board and presented it to him. Ms. Mendez repeated this procedure each time the topic changed and found that Joseph required fewer redirections and responded to questions and instructions more appropriately.

*Social Engagement—Preferred Activity*

## SOCIAL ENGAGEMENT

Social engagement can be described as active participation in classroom activities. Students evidence this skill by responding to social initiations and questions from others, expressing individual wants and needs, and interacting with peers. The social skills deficits characteristic of students with ASD include impairments in these skill areas and often result in the delayed development of interpersonal relationships (APA, 2000). Instead of engaging with others, these students are often content to spend excessive amounts of time engaged in self-stimulatory behaviors while avoiding other, more social activities (Schreibman, 2005). Because successful inclusion requires the ability to socialize and participate in a variety of interactive tasks, these deficits must be addressed. Requiring responses to questions, encouraging the student to make choices, and facilitating interaction with peers are several ways to enhance social engagement and can be embellished by additional teacher structure and clarity.

## Requiring Responses

Teachers can encourage social engagement by simply asking questions throughout instructional activities and facilitating responses through the use of prompts and social reinforcement. As students with ASD begin responding to social interactions initiated by others, the probability that communication and joint attention will occur increases. As a result, these students become more aware of others and learn that they are expected to respond (Whalen & Schreibman, 2003). As this process occurs, the teacher can begin decreasing prompts and thinning the schedule of reinforcement required during the acquisition of those skills.

> *Example:* During story time, one teacher found that students with autism were helped to be engaged with a task by frequently being asked simple questions about the information presented, such as, "What color is the bear?" or "How many monkeys are on the bed?" She also found that their attention increased when she checked for understanding by asking questions that required the students to immediately repeat a piece of information. For example, during calendar, she engaged a student by saying, "Today is Monday. Holly, what day is today?" Having the class respond in unison and using choral readings are effective variations of this technique that enhance the engagement of all students.

## Encouraging Choice Making

Reinhartsen, Garfinkle, and Wolery (2002) found that children's engagement in free play increased when they chose their toys. Favorable results were also found when students were given choices during teacher-assigned tasks; disruptive behaviors were reported to decrease while engagement increased (Moes, 1998). Those strategies have also been adapted to increase social engagement of students with ASD during instruction in inclusive settings, and have been found to be beneficial. During more structured work periods in which educational objectives were clearly specified, engagement was increased by allowing students to choose their own materials (i.e., crayon or marker; paper or white board). When participating in less structured activities, such as free centers, students were allowed to select the actual tasks that constituted their visual schedules. To monitor progress, students' engagement can be measured according to the duration or frequency of appropriate use of materials and the frequency of competing behaviors.

> *Example:* Billy, a 5-year-old with autism, had no difficulty during free centers but resisted more structured academic tasks. He was particularly resistant during mathematics, so his teacher encouraged choices within the math activities by allowing him to select both work materials, such as manipulative teddy bears or dinosaurs, for a counting

activity and the sequence of assignments. When he was given some control in making choices, his attention to academic tasks increased and his resistance decreased.

## Facilitating Peer Interaction

Facilitating interactions with typically developing peers also enhances social engagement. Reinhartsen et al. (2002) found that this outcome is more effectively accomplished when children are actively engaged in choosing the task; therefore, teachers may find students with autism are benefited by choosing activities and then having peers join in. Most likely, a preferred and familiar activity will be chosen, allowing the students to invest more attention in the interaction.

*Example:* Ms. Mendez found that her students with autism excel in completing puzzles, and they seem to enjoy sequencing tasks. She facilitated interaction among these students and their general education peers by having them complete an alphabet floor puzzle together. Prompting the students with autism to request the next letter in sequence or respond to peers' questions, such as "What's next?" enhanced their communication with peers, as demonstrated by the number of responses given and the duration of shared attention to the task.

## PHYSICAL ENGAGEMENT

Students demonstrate physical engagement in classroom activities by maintaining appropriate body posture and correctly using materials related to the task at hand. However, children with autism commonly engage in repetitive motor movements with their hands or their whole bodies (APA, 2000). During tasks that require sitting and listening, which are common in general education classrooms, these stereotypical behaviors are more likely to occur and result in decreased attention to task. Students with ASD can be physically engaged by providing an appropriate object to hold, incorporating opportunities to move, and including observation and imitation activities.

## Providing Objects to Hold

One suggested practice that reduces stereotypical behaviors and engages students with ASD is the provision of an appropriate object to hold (Dahle, 2003). Giving the student a small item, such as a squishy ball, to hold and reinforcing the alternative behavior at varying intervals can be helpful in decreasing inappropriate hand movements. This approach, however, can be distracting to some students, so the use of manipulative materials that reflect the task at hand may be more beneficial.

*Social Engagement—Imitation*

*Example:* Daniel's struggle with circle time included difficulty controlling self-stimulatory hand movements. To remedy this problem, Miss Cowley created a handheld replica of the calendar bulletin board using Velcro to attach the days, months, and weather conditions. When talking about today, she prompted Daniel to move the correct icon to the "today" space in his book as she moved the card on the bulletin board. To assess the effectiveness of this intervention, a classroom aide took a weekly tally of the number of times self-stimulatory behaviors occurred during circle time, and found that as Daniel's independence in using these materials increased, the frequency of his self-stimulatory behaviors decreased.

## Incorporating Opportunities for Movement

Throughout activities that require extensive sitting and listening, students with autism are helped by being given opportunities to move about. As a result, the students become actively engaged in the group activity and are less likely to withdraw. One way to accomplish this end is by having them assist in completing simple tasks that permit them to leave their seats and act as "teacher's helpers."

*Example:* Ms. Mendez noticed that Alan had difficulty sitting still and attending to instructional activities. To address this issue, she incor-

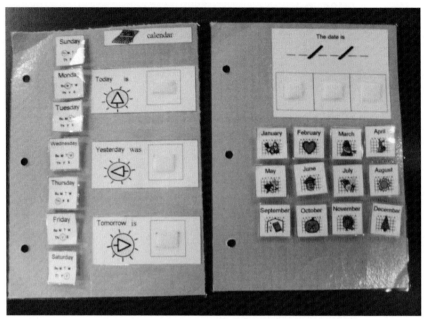

*Calendar Book Pages*

porated ways to allow him to physically assist her. For example, when reading a story to the class, Ms. Mendez allowed Alan to turn pages when instructed. During calendar activities, she had him point to the days of the week as the class sang. When it was another student's turn to act as calendar helper, she encouraged Alan's involvement by asking him to "Please give the pointer to Matthew." By affording him brief opportunities to move about and assist in group activities, Ms. Mendez found that Alan was less withdrawn and more attentive.

## Including Imitation Activities

Finally, the ability to imitate is a core deficit for children with autism and is important to address, because it is related to play, communication, and other social behaviors (Schreibman, 2005). Increasing engagement can be further accomplished by including activities that focus on the development of this skill, because naturalistic imitation training had been shown to result in gains in object imitation, spontaneous language, and joint attention (Ingersoll & Schreibman, 2006). Incorporating imitation in classroom activities increases student engagement and is evidenced as the observation of, and response to, others' actions.

*Example:* Some teachers incorporate books that encourage movement during story time, for example, *From Head to Toe* by Eric Carle

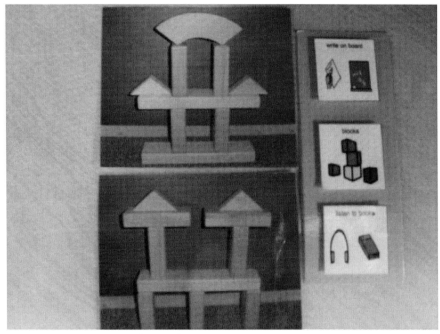

*Centers Schedule and Block Models*

(1997). Others have used music to engage students, for instance, by encouraging imitative actions through dance. As students develop imitation skills during structured activities, the teacher can then shift the focus to encouraging the imitation of prosocial behaviors during other activities.

## FINAL THOUGHTS

In summary, the intervention strategies suggested here are intended to be unobtrusive methods for increasing the probability that students with ASD will maintain academic engagement in instructional activities. The normalized behaviors promoted by these strategies are likely to determine whether the inclusion of these students in general education classrooms is successful. An important point to note is that many of the interventions recommended are useful for increasing the engagement of all students, both those with ASD and other class members, because they are used during group activities in which all students participate. Other interventions are individually prescribed but can be adapted for use with any student who has an attention deficit, regardless of whether the student is identified with ASD. Evidence has long shown (Kounin, 1966) that teachers who are most effective in managing the behavior of general education students are also more effective in managing the behavior of students with behavioral issues. Most of the strategies recommended here are thus designed for increasing teacher effectiveness in general as well as increasing the engagement of individual students with ASD. To be successful with either group, however, several points must be considered in the implementation of these strategies.

First, engagement strategies must expressly be taught to these students. Such direct instruction is especially important for students with autism because they are not as likely as others to vicariously acquire social and academic skills. They also do not typically respond to traditional verbal instruction and may require prompting (Harrower & Dunlap, 2001). Children with autism commonly require full physical assistance when acquiring new social and academic skills. Paraprofessionals or teacher aides are especially helpful during the acquisition phase of skill development, and their assistance can gradually be faded as students become more proficient.

Second, a great variation of skill levels exists among students with autism, and significant differences may be evident in the amount of time required for particular students to demonstrate independence in strategy use. Generally, interventions should be implemented and monitored for a 4- to 6-week period. If the student is demonstrating progress, the teaching phase of the intervention should be continued until independent performance on the part of the student is exhibited and maintained through the naturally occurring reinforcement in the classroom environment. If the student is not progressing after this period, a different strategy should be designed and implemented.

Generalization strategies will be necessary for students with ASD who are being integrated into inclusive classrooms. In this situation, an IAT, a special education consultant, or a special education co-teacher may be required to analyze the receiving environment to assure that the student has mastered the skills required for successful participation and that the receiving general education teacher has the necessary instructional materials and teaching skills to implement the interventions. Such an individual can make certain that previously acquired engagement strategies are maintained in the inclusive environment.

Finally, the interventions suggested here should not be viewed as constituting a finite list of recommendations for increasing the engagement of the group of diverse students labeled with ASD. Intervention strategies must be viewed as fluid and evolving rather than static. They are most effective when special and general education teachers first collaborate in a problem-solving analysis that evaluates students' unique engagement deficits and then develop individually designed interventions that are linked with the unique requirements of a specific class activity. As a result, the intervention strategies field-tested in these inclusive settings are processes that provide general guidelines and structure for prescribing others that increase the engagement of students with ASD. Furthermore, these strategies, although presented in isolation, are often more effective when used in conjunction with one another. For example, during circle-time activities, the teacher is encouraged to increase auditory engagement by singing about the days of the week, to increase visual and physical engagement by providing a calendar book with movable icons, and to increase social engagement by asking questions about the information presented. This comprehensive approach may be challenging to implement, but it will result in success for both the teacher and the student with autism.

# REFERENCES

Alberto, P., & Troutman, A. (2003). *Applied behavior analysis for teachers* (6th ed.). Upper Saddle River, NJ: Prentice-Hall.

American Psychiatric Association. (APA). (2000). *Diagnostic and statistical manual of mental disorders—text revision* (4th ed.). Washington, DC: Author.

Carle, E. (1997). *From head to toe.* New York: Scholastic.

Centers for Disease Control and Prevention. (2006). *How common are autism spectrum disorders (ASD)?* Retrieved July 11, 2006, from http://www.cdc.gov/ncbddd/autism/asd_common.htm

Dahle, K. B. (2003). Services to include young children with autism in the general classroom. *Early Childhood Education Journal, 31,* 65–70.

Dettmer, S., Simpson, R. L., Myles, B., & Ganz, J. B. (2000). The use of visual supports to facilitate transitions of students with autism. *Focus on Autism and Other Developmental Disabilities, 15,* 163–169.

Donnellan, A. M., Mesaros, R. A., & Anderson, J. L. (1984). Teaching students with autism in natural environments: What educators need from researchers. *Journal of Special Education, 18,* 505–522.

Fisher, M., & Meyer, L. H. (2002). Development and social competence after two years for students enrolled in inclusive and self-contained educational programs. *Research and Practice for Persons with Severe Disabilities, 27,* 165–174.

Grandin, T. (2002). *Teaching tips for children and adults with autism.* Retrieved July 11, 2006, from http://www.autism.org/temple/tips.html

Harrower, J. K., & Dunlap, G. (2001). Including children with autism in general education classrooms: A review of effective strategies. *Behavior Modification, 25,* 762–784.

Ingersoll, B., & Schreibman, L. (2006). Teaching reciprocal imitation skills to young children with autism using a naturalistic approach: Effects on language, pretend play, and joint attention. *Journal of Autism and Developmental Disorders, 36,* 487–505.

Kaplan, R. S., & Steele, A. L. (2005). An analysis of music therapy program goals and outcomes for clients with diagnoses on the autism spectrum. *Journal of Music Therapy, 42,* 2–19.

Kounin, J. S. (1966). Managing emotionally disturbed children in regular classrooms. *Journal of Educational Psychology, 57,* 1–13.

Kounin, J. S. (1977). *Discipline and group management in classrooms.* Huntington, NY: R. E. Krieger.

Landry, R., & Bryson, S. E. (2004). Impaired disengagement of attention in young children with autism. *Journal of Child Psychology and Psychiatry, 45,* 1115–1122.

Marks, S. U., Shaw-Hegwer, J., Schrader, C., Longaker, T., Peters, I., Powers, F., et al. (2003). Instructional management tips for teachers of students with autism spectrum disorder (ASD). *TEACHING Exceptional Children, 35,* 50–55.

Moes, D. (1998). Integrating choice-making opportunities within teacher-assigned academic tasks to facilitate the performance of children with autism. *Journal of the Association for Persons With Severe Handicaps, 23,* 319–328.

Quill, K. A. (1995). Visually cued instruction for children with autism and pervasive developmental disorders. *Focus on Autistic Behavior, 10,* 10–20.

Reinhartsen, D. B., Garfinkle, A. N., & Wolery, M. (2002). Engagement with toys in two-year-old children with autism: Teacher selection versus child choice. *Research and Practice for Persons with Severe Disabilities, 27,* 175–187.

Rogers, S. J. (2000). Interventions that facilitate socialization in children with autism. *Journal of Autism and Developmental Disorders, 30,* 399–409.

Schreibman, L. (2005). *The science and fiction of autism.* Cambridge, MA: Harvard University Press.

Shapiro, E. S. (2004). *Academic skills problems: Direct assessment and intervention* (3rd ed.). New York: Guilford Press.

Treatment and Education of Autistic and Related Communication-handicapped Children. (2004). *TEACCH classroom training program.* Chapel Hill, NC: University of North Carolina.

Watanabe, M., & Sturmey, P. (2003). The effect of choice-making opportunities during activity schedules on task engagement of adults with autism. *Journal of Autism and Developmental Disorders, 33,* 535–538.

Whalen, C., & Schreibman, L. (2003). Joint attention training for children with autism using behavior modification procedures. *Journal of Child Psychology and Psychiatry and Allied Disciplines, 44,* 456–468.

Originally published in *TEACHING Exceptional Children,* Vol. 39, No. 6, pp. 53–61.

# 3

# Using Structured Work Systems to Promote Independence and Engagement for Students With Autism Spectrum Disorders

Christi R. Carnahan, Kara Hume, Laura Clarke, and Christy Borders

*Mrs. Bonds was the district autism specialist. She, along with teachers, thera-pists, and paraprofessionals, supported students with autism spectrum disor-ders (ASD) in preschool through 12th grade, across general and special education settings. Though the skills of the students she served varied tremen-dously, she noticed a common difficulty for many of her students with ASD, despite age or functioning level: a broad deficit in independent functioning. This impacted her youngest students as they learned basic school readiness skills, including gathering and putting away materials, or completing a basic sequence of activities, such as coloring, cutting, and gluing. This same diffi-culty made it hard for her older students to follow more complex response chains and manage all of their belongings, materials, and assignments throughout the day. Mrs. Bonds needed an intervention that could address this difficulty, one that would be appropriate for a variety of students in a number of settings. After careful review of evidence-based practices and discussion with colleagues, she decided to implement **work systems,** an element of struc-tured teaching developed by Division TEACCH, with several of her students.*

An important goal for all students is the ability to function independently throughout the school day—moving from one location to the next, organizing required materials, completing necessary tasks, and applying skills learned in one setting to other settings when appropriate. Although this goal is a priority for all students, it is even more important for students with ASD, as independence is the key to successful community inclusion and future employment. In a study of 68 adults with autism with IQs measured above 50, two thirds were not employed and only 3 lived independently, likely due to the well-documented difficulties in independent performance (Howlin, Goode, Hutton, & Rutter, 2004). This difficulty in independent performance has been recognized as a programming priority by many in the field (Lord & McGee, 2001; Olley, 1999). Lord and McGee identified "independent organizational skills . . . such as completing a task independently" as one of eight recommended educational objectives for students with autism (p. 218). Olley noted that "the goals of all curricula and methods are to assist students to work independently" (p. 602).

The development of independent skills is an essential curricular goal for students with ASD; it is also essential that staff like Mrs. Bonds who support students with ASD understand the complex skills required for independent performance. In addition, it is helpful to understand what challenges students with ASD may face when developing and demonstrating the skills necessary to complete an activity on their own.

• • • • • • • • • • • • • • • • • • • • • • • • • • • • • • • • • • • • • • • • • • • • • • • • • • • • • • • • •

*Mrs. Bonds wanted to implement an intervention that would really work; her first step was to try to better understand why independent performance was so hard for her students, even those who were fully included in academic classes. She wanted to know how her students thought and what was impeding their progress.*

• • • • • • • • • • • • • • • • • • • • • • • • • • • • • • • • • • • • • • • • • • • • • • • • • • • • • • • • •

## LEARNING NEEDS IN STUDENTS WITH ASD

*Active engagement* is one of the strongest predictors of learning for students with ASD (Iovannone, Dunlap, Huber, & Kincaid, 2003; R. Koegel, Koegel, & McNerney, 2001). When actively engaged, people attend to, recognize, analyze, and store important details or information (Quill, 2000), and then use these details to construct meaning (i.e., integrate information for meaningful purposes). However, traditional teaching techniques such as lectures or lengthy verbal instructions may limit or inhibit engagement and independence of students with ASD (Carnahan, 2006). These techniques may not take into consideration the unique needs of students with ASD in the areas of attention, organization and sequencing, initiation, and generalization (Rao & Gagie, 2006).

### Attention

Many individuals with autism are unable to attend to multiple stimuli or environmental cues (Quill, 2000). These individuals demonstrate *stimulus overselectivity* (Reed & Gibson, 2005), or attention to a limited number of environmental cues at one time. Students with ASD may attend to specific parts or aspects of a situation without regard for the context within which the situation occurs (Happe & Frith, 2006; Quill). Overselective attention, or attention to parts rather than wholes, limits an individual's ability to understand the "big picture" (Happe & Frith, p. 6). This is especially true as task demands increase or situations become more complex (Reed & Gibson). This difference in attention may influence students' abilities to perform independently as they may not attend to all of the steps required for task completion, such as missing the directive to put one's name on a paper before turning it in. Similarly, students may not understand how completion of an independent routine fits into the larger school day. For example, the student may not see how his difficulty gathering his books at the end of the day before boarding the bus may impact the entire bus schedule.

## Organization and Sequencing

Completing an activity from start to finish is challenging for many individuals with ASD, a result of differences in organizing and sequencing information from the environment. Organizing and sequencing require *dual focus*, the ability to know what has to be completed first (or next), while simultaneously understanding the relationship between steps and what the end result should look like. Students with ASD may not be able to determine how to approach a situation, identify exactly what needs to be done, and set an appropriate goal or plan. They may not be able to identify the tasks to accomplish or determine where to start, and may not be able to sequence and implement specific steps to achieve a goal, especially when facing other distractions (Fisher & Happe, 2005). Because they appear not to know what to do, students with ASD often require additional prompts, or are reprimanded for not completing a task.

Consider the task of organizing a desk or work space, a job that most school staff expect students to complete independently and rather quickly. The ability to organize and sequence information from the environment is crucial to completing such a task. In order to organize the desk area, students need to identify the problem (e.g., papers are not getting home, homework is missing); set a goal (e.g., put all homework in the red folder, throw away dated materials); and develop a plan to meet the goal. After establishing a plan, the student gathers the necessary supplies (e.g., folders, pencil case) and begins organizing. For students with ASD, this task may be overwhelming and immobilizing.

## Initiation

Individuals with ASD often do not independently initiate the completion of steps during classroom activities (L. Koegel, Carter, & Koegel, 2003; R. Koegel et al., 2001). Though students may have learned a school-based routine, such as getting out the science materials required for a lab activity or the steps followed when checking out a library book, prompts may still be required to initiate each part of the routine. Individuals with ASD often learn to wait for prompts, which impedes initiation and independent functioning. This difficulty with initiation is likely impacted as well by their difficulties with attention, organization, and sequencing.

## Generalization

Many individuals with ASD have difficulty generalizing skills learned in one environment to new environments (L. Koegel, Koegel, Harrower, & Carter, 1999). They may also demonstrate behavioral differences from one setting to another (Lord & McGee, 2001). Many individuals with ASD demonstrate a detail-oriented processing style, focusing on specific details of an event, routine, or concept, without connecting the details that create meaning (Happe & Frith, 2006). Focusing on specific details without attention to the bigger picture causes an individual to miss the central principles or components that would allow generalization of skills across environments (Hume, 2004).

••••••••••••••••••••••••••••••••••••••••••••••••••••••••••••••••••••••••••••••••

*Mrs. Bonds could certainly relate to all that she read about the attention, organization, sequencing, and initiation of individuals with ASD. It was her reading about generalization difficulties, however, that highlighted a number of the challenges her students faced relating to independence. She thought in particular about Jacob, a third grader with ASD. Although Jacob was able to unpack his backpack when he arrived at school, he was unable to repack it at the end of the day as he prepared to ride the bus home—despite the fact that the routine was the same, just reversed. After reading about generalization difficulties, Mrs. Bonds understood why Jacob was having difficulty with the independent performance of his afternoon routine: In the morning, a paraprofessional was in the classroom and provided the initial verbal prompt, "unpack your bag," followed with proximity prompts. As Jacob took each item out of his backpack, she moved in the direction of the bin, shelf, or folder where the item belonged. For example, as Jacob took out his lunch bag, she stepped toward the large bin designated for packed lunches. Jacob paid close attention to these prompts; in fact, he attended more to her proximity than to the items he took out of his bag or the designated locations. Jacob missed the principle of "unpacking" his bag. Without this staff member in place, Jacob was not able to perform the routine, even though he was very familiar with each step.*

••••••••••••••••••••••••••••••••••••••••••••••••••••••••••••••••••••••••••••••••

Difficulties in generalizing behaviors and detail-oriented processing significantly influence the ability of individuals with ASD to participate independently in many different environments. Specifically, these characteristics may lead to overreliance on adult prompting and decrease the potential for independence at school and in the community (Mesibov, Shea, & Schopler, 2005).

••••••••••••••••••••••••••••••••••••••••••••••••••••••••••••••••••••••

*Mrs. Bonds was ready to select an intervention that would support student independence and assist in remedying the difficulties her students were facing. After reading several journal articles (Dettmer, Simpson, Smith-Myles, & Ganz, 2000; Hume & Odom, 2007), she decided that work systems would benefit her students in a variety of settings across a number of skills.*

••••••••••••••••••••••••••••••••••••••••••••••••••••••••••••••••••••••

## WHAT IS A WORK SYSTEM?

A work system, an element of structured teaching developed by Division TEACCH, is a visually organized system designed to promote understanding and clarity for individuals with ASD (Hume & Odom, 2007; see boxes, "What Does the Research Say About Work Systems?" and "What Is Division TEACCH?"). Work systems rely on predictability and clarity to promote understanding of the environment and expectations (Mesibov et al., 2005), and offer a tool for assisting students with ASD in focusing on important details, maintaining attention to tasks, and generalizing skills learned in one setting to new environments. Specifically, work systems provide specific directions about *what to do* (e.g., sequence of activities) in a given area of the classroom or school building, while also providing a *systematic work routine*—working from left to right or top to bottom. Work systems can be used in a variety of settings and for a variety of purposes, including routines that occur throughout the school day, independent work time, and small-group lessons. The goal of a work system is to organize tasks and activities in ways that are comprehensible to students with ASD. This systematic and organized presentation of tasks and materials visually answers four important questions (Mesibov et al.):

1. What activities do I complete?

2. How many activities do I complete?

3. How will I know when the work is finished?

4. What will happen after the work is complete?

Using visual organization, work systems meet the needs of students with ASD and similar learning characteristics in several ways; they

- Highlight important information and help limit distractions.

- Offer clear and predictable sequences of activities.

- Minimize the need for verbal instructions.

- Minimize the need for adult prompting.

**What Does the Research Say About Work Systems?**

Recent research has demonstrated the efficacy of the work system in increasing on-task behavior and productivity in three students with autism, while decreasing the number of prompts required from adults (Hume & Odom, 2007). To reduce transition time and adult prompting, Dettmer, Simpson, Smith-Myles, and Ganz (2000) incorporated several elements of an individual work system (e.g., finished box, pictorial cues) in another study involving three children with autism. The supports were successful in reducing latency between instruction and student response and in decreasing adult prompting. Additional studies have shown the effectiveness of structured teaching methods for (a) promoting the independent performance of children with autism and severe intellectual disability during work sessions and transitions (Panerai, Ferrante, & Caputo, 1997); (b) reducing self-injurious behavior (Norgate, 1998); and (c) increasing the vocational skills in individuals entering the job market (Keel, Mesibov, & Woods, 1997). Several studies have compared the TEACCH program with other interventions (Ozonoff & Cathcart, 1998; Panerai, Ferrante, & Zingale, 2002), and shows statistically significant gains in all areas on the Psychoeducational Profile-Revised (PEP-R; Schopler, Reichler, Bashford, Lansing, & Marcus, 1990).

## IMPLEMENTING A WORK SYSTEM

All work systems tell the student what to do first, next, and last. However, the unique needs of each student will guide decisions about the type of system to use. Structured work systems can have simple or complex designs and can be concrete or abstract, as long as the design aligns with the skills and attributes of the individuals using them. The design of an individual work system for a student who does not yet read or write will be different from the design of a work system for someone who is able to read and comprehend written directions. Similarly, the work systems of students who are able to travel from one area to another without adult support will look different than work systems designed for students who require adult prompts to move from one area to another.

**What Is Division TEACCH?**

Division TEACCH (Treatment and Education of Autistic and Related Communication Handicapped Children; www.teacch.com) is a comprehensive statewide program based at the University of North Carolina at Chapel Hill and serves children and adults on the autism spectrum. Founded in the early 1970s, Division TEACCH provides services to individuals with ASD and their families, conducts training worldwide on effective teaching practices, and participates in research activities.

## Prioritize Student Needs

The first step in designing a work system is to determine what activities or routines require independence. Possibilities in the school environment include completing several academic or leisure tasks independently, going through the cafeteria line, or using a vending machine.

• • • • • • • • • • • • • • • • • • • • • • • • • • • • • • • • • • • • • • • • • • • • • • • • • • • • • • • • •

*Mrs. Bonds decided that Jacob's need to pack his backpack was certainly a priority; his difficulty resulted in frequent tardiness to the bus, which led to great frustration for the bus driver and other students.*

• • • • • • • • • • • • • • • • • • • • • • • • • • • • • • • • • • • • • • • • • • • • • • • • • • • • • • • • •

## Choose Work System Format

The next step is to choose the type of presentation for the work system. For a concrete learner with beginning-level skills, a left-to-right work system will likely be most appropriate (see Figure 1). The system teaches the student to move items from left to right as they are completed. All of the items needed to complete the activity should be arranged before the student arrives to the assigned location, and organized in containers, folders, envelopes, trays, or shelves. On the student's right should be a location for completed or finished materials (Dettmer et al., 2000; Schopler, Reichler, Bashford, Lansing, & Marcus, 1990)—a "finished" box, basket, shelf, or table. In addition, the work space should include visual information (e.g., object, picture, word) about what activity the student will be participating in next (Schopler et al.).

Left-to-right and other more sophisticated work systems (see Figure 2) can be used throughout the school day—during academic activities, language groups, independent work times, and across age ranges. Work systems are helpful for older students who are able to match and sequence activities, yet still struggle with organizational skills. The use of a matching work system or a list work system may be most meaningful to some students with ASD. Instead of a student using or completing all of the materials/tasks on the left, a matching or written work system indicates exactly what activities will be completed and in what order. Matching and written work systems can be used in a variety of activities in the classroom and community.

## Teach the Student the Work System

Once the work system is set up for the student, staff should teach the student how to use the system. It is important to ensure that any adults providing prompts (and the prompts themselves) do not become part of the work routine for the student. Staff should stand quietly behind the student while prompting to ensure that the work system materials (rather than the adult and/or prompts themselves) are in the student's view. Follow a least-to-most prompting hierarchy (Repp, Karsh, & Lenz, 1990), first presenting the work

**Figure 1. Left-to-Right Work Systems**

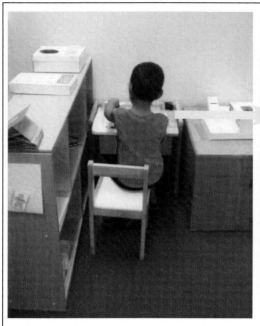 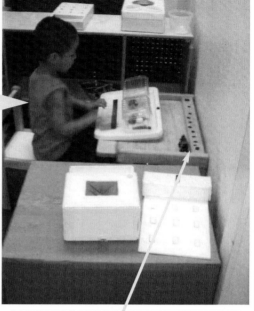

The toy train indicates that he will go to the play area when he is finished.

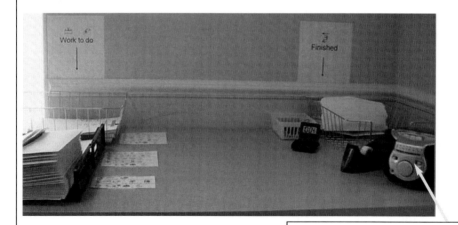

The CD player indicates that he can listen to music when he is finished.

**Figure 2. Matching and Written Work Systems**

Example A

Matching work systems (see Example A) are more sophisticated than left-to-right systems in that they require an individual to be able to match attributes (e.g., color, number, shape, pictures, etc.). A Velcro strip is affixed to the student's work space and activity areas (i.e., individual desk, small group table, restroom, etc.) and contains numbers, letters, pictures, and so forth, that correspond to designated activities. The student takes the first icon and matches it to the corresponding activity. After completing the designated activity, the student obtains the next icon and moves it to the corresponding activity. The last item on the list tells the student what to do after completing the task.

The student takes the top letter and matches it to the corresponding folder on the left. Once all of the letters are matched and the activities are completed, the student transitions to the activity indicated at the end of the work system.

The student takes the top number and matches it to the corresponding shelf on the left. Once all of the numbers are matched and the activities are completed, the student transitions to the activity at the end of the work system.

A written work system also answers the four work system questions for students. The written list (see Example B) describes both what activities need to be completed and how many activities need to be completed. Students are provided with an overview of all required activities, and learn that they are finished when each activity is crossed off. Students may use a finished box or may replace materials when they are finished.

Example B

1. Enter returned books into computer

2. Return box of books to shelf.

3. Return books on tables in children's section

4. Surf the Internet until 3:15 PM

READING GROUP

1. Read pages 1-15 in "Legends" book _____
2. Answer questions on worksheet _____
3. Raise hand to have teacher check answers _____
4. Computer _____

**Figure 3. Jacob's Left-to-Right Work System for Packing His Backpack**

Mrs. Bonds placed a desk in the classroom's backpack area. On the desk (see photograph) she placed Jacob's lunchbox, his homework folder, his baseball from recess, PTA flyers, and his textbooks—all of the items he often neglected packing at the end of the school day. To the right of the desk she placed his backpack, already unzipped, to serve as his "finished" box. She wrote "Bus" on a sticky note that she placed on the far right side of the desk.

Upon arrival to his backpack work system, Jacob was visually able to answer the four work system questions. He was able to scan the work system area and identify what activity was to be completed (packing his backpack) and how many items needed to be placed in the backpack (the items on the left). He could understand when packing his backpack would be finished (when all of the items on the left of the desk were placed in his backpack and his desk was empty), and it was clear what activity was going to occur next (getting on the bus).

system materials to offer assistance (e.g., the task, the finished box); then providing a nonverbal, gestural prompt; moving next to a verbal prompt; and finally providing physical assistance if needed. If verbal prompts are necessary instructions should be concise.

••••••••••••••••••••••••••••••••••••••••••••••••••••••••••••••••••••

*Mrs. Bonds decided that the left-to-right work system was a perfect fit for Jacob's backpack packing intervention (see Figure 3). Though the work system required some minimal set-up by a staff person or peer, Jacob was quickly able to learn the work system routine and could pack his backpack quickly and independently.*

••••••••••••••••••••••••••••••••••••••••••••••••••••••••••••••••••••

## Collect Data

A final and essential step in the implementation process is collecting data on student performance in the use of the work system. Data may be collected on the level of prompting required for the student to successfully manipulate the work system (see Figure 4). In addition, it is recommended that staff collect data on the target behaviors that served as the impetus for work system implementation (e.g., overreliance on adult prompting, off-task behavior, low productivity). These data may be collected and graphed so staff can make informed decisions about the success of the strategy (See Figure 5).

In collecting data on student use of a matching work system in math class, for example, Task 1 may be a measuring activity in the textbook and Task 2 may be a measuring work sheet. The student would receive a score of "6" on "Approaches Task" for Task 1 for independently matching the letter from the work system to the letter on Task 1. If she has difficulty beginning the task and the teacher needs to point to the textbook to help her get started, then she would receive a score of "4" for "Begins Task." The student would receive a score of "6" for "Completes Task" if able to complete the task without further prompts. Finally, a student who requires physical assistance to place the activity back in the lettered folder would receive a score of "2" for "What's Next." The goal is for adult prompting to decrease over time as the student becomes more proficient in the use of the work system. Scores should move from low scores, indicating a low level of independence (and high level of prompting) to high scores, indicating a high level of independence.

• • • • • • • • • • • • • • • • • • • • • • • • • • • • • • • • • • • • • • • • • • • • • • • • • • • • • •

*The issues Jacob faced regarding organization, sequencing, initiation, attention, and generalization were alleviated and the data on Jacob's work system indicated that he was able to complete the steps independently for almost 90% of the opportunities.*

• • • • • • • • • • • • • • • • • • • • • • • • • • • • • • • • • • • • • • • • • • • • • • • • • • • • • •

## ADAPTING WORK SYSTEMS TO STUDENT NEEDS

Mrs. Bonds was so pleased with Jacob's response to the left-to-right work system that she was eager to try the same intervention with another student. Kate was a middle school student with ASD who struggled when it was time to practice a newly taught skill. Her math teacher would teach a skill; after practicing in small groups, students were expected to complete two or three tasks on their own to generalize the skill. Kate often just sat during this time because she missed some of the verbal directions and had difficulty locating all of the required materials. Mrs. Bonds decided to implement a matching work system for Kate that could assist in clarifying what activities were to be completed and in what order. She set up a series of folders labeled with letters on a shelf near Kate's desk. Each folder contained materials required for the independent math activities, such as a ruler and worksheet, a calculator

**Figure 4. Sample Data Sheet**

**Work System**

Student's Name:                                        **Work System:**

Information Provided

___ What work?      ___ How much work?      ___ When finished?      ___ What next?

| TASK #1 | Approaches task | Begins task | Completes task | What next? |
|---------|-----------------|-------------|----------------|------------|
|         | 6               | 6           | 6              | 6          |
|         | 5               | 5           | 5              | 5          |
|         | 4               | 4           | 4              | 4          |
|         | 3               | 3           | 3              | 3          |
|         | 2               | 2           | 2              | 2          |
|         | 1               | 1           | 1              | 1          |

| TASK #2 | Approaches task | Begins task | Completes task | What next? |
|---------|-----------------|-------------|----------------|------------|
|         | 6               | 6           | 6              | 6          |
|         | 5               | 5           | 5              | 5          |
|         | 4               | 4           | 4              | 4          |
|         | 3               | 3           | 3              | 3          |
|         | 2               | 2           | 2              | 2          |
|         | 1               | 1           | 1              | 1          |

| TASK #3 | Approaches task | Begins task | Completes task | What next? |
|---------|-----------------|-------------|----------------|------------|
|         | 6               | 6           | 6              | 6          |
|         | 5               | 5           | 5              | 5          |
|         | 4               | 4           | 4              | 4          |
|         | 3               | 3           | 3              | 3          |
|         | 2               | 2           | 2              | 2          |
|         | 1               | 1           | 1              | 1          |

| TASK #4 | Approaches task | Begins task | Completes task | What next? |
|---------|-----------------|-------------|----------------|------------|
|         | 6               | 6           | 6              | 6          |
|         | 5               | 5           | 5              | 5          |
|         | 4               | 4           | 4              | 4          |
|         | 3               | 3           | 3              | 3          |
|         | 2               | 2           | 2              | 2          |
|         | 1               | 1           | 1              | 1          |

**Code**

| 1 = Fail | 3 = Verbal Prompt | 5 = Material Prompt |
|----------|-------------------|---------------------|
| 2 = Physical Prompt | 4 = Gestural Prompt | 6 = Independent |

*Note.* Data sheet developed by Division TEACCH (Ament, 1999) to track student usage of independent work systems. Data are collected on level of adult prompting. Adult prompting should decrease over time (moving from physical prompts, if needed, to independence).

**Figure 5. Data Collected by Division TEACCH to Track Kalif's Usage of Independent Work Systems**

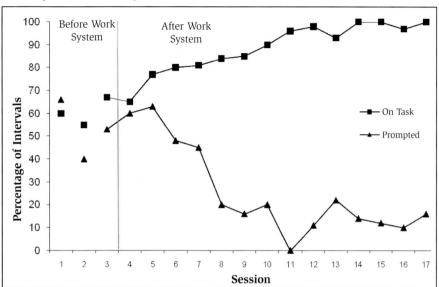

and textbook, or word problems and manipulatives. On Kate's desk Mrs. Bonds placed a small strip of paper with the same letters to indicate what folders Kate should use that day. In addition, Mrs. Bonds wrote a note about what activity Kate would transition to when those math activities were finished. Mrs. Bonds also decided that Kate didn't need a separate finished basket, as she understood that abstract concept. Instead, Kate was taught to put the materials back in the folder where she found them.

Mrs. Bonds tried another work system with a high school student, Kalif, who had difficulty when he went to his job at the local public library. He was able to arrive and punch in independently, but then typically relied on a job coach or co-worker to get started on each task. Though he knew how to do each job, he required assistance in initiating the activity and understanding the order in which activities should be completed. He was often off task while he waited for prompts. The tasks varied from day to day, needed to be finished in a specific order, and required organization and sequencing. Mrs. Bonds could have used a left-to-right work system by setting up the required tasks, such as filing and stamping books, on his left and a finished shelf on the right, or a matching work system, by labeling each activity with a visual cue and giving Kalif corresponding cues. Instead, because of Kalif's ability to read, comprehend, and follow a numbered list, Mrs. Bonds decided to set up a written list work system. After punching in, Kalif received a list of three tasks he was to complete while working at the library. When he was finished with each task, he crossed it off the list, and moved to the next one. At the end of the list was a written cue directing Kalif to the next activity, which was typically something he enjoyed. This provided additional motivation for Kalif to complete his work in a timely way.

## FINAL THOUGHTS

The changes in Mrs. Bonds's students were similar to those documented in the research (Hume & Odom, 2007). Her data indicated that the students using work systems demonstrated higher levels of independent functioning, measured by increases in on-task behavior and decreases in adult prompting (Figure 5 reflects Kalif's data). In addition, she noted that students were generalizing more effectively when work systems were in place across setting. Anecdotally, she reported that productivity was rising, as her students began to better understand how many tasks or activities were required, when they would be finished, and learn to anticipate a following activity. As her students progressed she began to increase the complexity of the work systems. For example, after Jacob mastered the left-to-right work system, Mrs. Bonds introduced a matching work system for packing his backpack. She hoped to eventually use a written work system as his literacy skills developed.

Independently moving through the school day is a crucial skill for students with ASD. Activities that other students seemingly find easy, such as transitioning from one location to the next, organizing learning materials, and completing assigned activities can be challenging for students with ASD. By using structured work systems, educators address the unique learning styles and challenges experienced by these students. Such systems provide concrete and meaningful information—increasing engagement and independence, decreasing anxiety, and ultimately helping students experience more success across settings. The steps described in this article offer educators a foundation for implementing work systems and preparing students for future success.

# REFERENCES

Ament, N. (1999, September). *Monitoring progress using the TEACCH model: Options and innovations.* Chapel Hill, NC: TEACCH Level II Training.

Carnahan, C. (2006). Engaging children with autism and their teachers. *TEACHING Exceptional Children, 39*(2), 44–50.

Dettmer, S., Simpson, R., Smith-Myles, B., & Ganz, J. (2000). The use of visual supports to facilitate transitions of students with autism. *Focus on Autism and Other Developmental Disabilities, 15,* 163–169.

Fisher, N., & Happe, F. (2005). A training study of theory of mind and executive function in children with autistic spectrum disorders. *Journal of Autism and Developmental Disorders, 35,* 757–771.

Happe, F., & Frith, U. (2006). The weak coherence account: Detail-focused cognitive style in autism spectrum disorders. *Journal of Autism and Developmental Disorders, 36,* 5–25.

Howlin, P., Goode, S., Hutton, J., & Rutter, M. (2004). Adult outcome for children with autism. *Journal of Child Psychology and Psychiatry, 45,* 212–229.

Hume, K. (2004, Fall). I can do it myself: Using work systems to build independence in students with autism spectrum disorders. *The Reporter, 10*(1), 4–6, 16.

Hume, K., & Odom, S. (2007). Effects of an individual work system on the independent engagement of students with autism. *Journal of Autism and Developmental Disorders, 37,* 1166–1180.

Iovannone, R., Dunlap, G., Huber, H., & Kincaid, D. (2003). Effective educational practices for students with autism spectrum disorders. *Focus on Autism and Other Developmental Disabilities, 18,* 150–165.

Keel, J., Mesibov, G., & Woods, A. (1997). TEACCH-supported employment program. *Journal of Autism and Developmental Disorders, 27,* 3–9.

Koegel, L., Carter, C., & Koegel, R. (2003). Teaching children with autism self-initiations as a pivotal response. *Topics in Language Disorders, 23,* 134–145.

Koegel, L., Koegel, R., Harrower, J., & Carter, C. (1999). Pivotal response intervention I: Overview of approach. *The Journal of the Association for Persons with Severe Handicaps, 24*(3), 174–185.

Koegel, R., Koegel, L., & McNerney, E. (2001). Pivotal areas in intervention for autism. *Journal of Clinical Child Psychology, 30,* 19–32.

Lord, C., & McGee, J. P. (Eds.). (2001). *Educating children with autism.* Washington, DC: National Academy Press.

Mesibov, G., Shea, V., & Schopler, E. (2005). *The TEACCH approach to autism spectrum disorders.* New York: Kluwer Academic/Plenum.

Norgate, R. (1998). Reducing self injurious behavior in a child with severe learning difficulties: Enhancing predictability and structure. *Educational Psychology in Practice, 14,* 176–182.

Olley, G. (1999). Curriculum for students with autism. *School Psychology Review, 28,* 595–608.

Ozonoff, S., & Cathcart, K. (1998). Effectiveness of a home program intervention for young children with autism. *Journal of Autism and Developmental Disorders, 28,* 25–32.

Panerai, S., Ferrante, L., & Caputo, V. (1997). The TEACCH strategy in mentally retarded children with autism: A multidimensional assessment. *Journal of Autism and Developmental Disorders, 27,* 345–347.

Panerai, S., Ferrante, L., & Zingale, M. (2002). Benefits of the treatment and education of autistic and communication handicapped children (TEACCH) programme as compared with a non-specific approach. *Journal of Intellectual Disability Research, 46,* 318–327.

Quill, K. A. (2000). *Do-watch-listen-say: Social and communication intervention for children with autism.* Baltimore: Paul H. Brookes.

Rao, S., & Gagie, B. (2006). Learning through seeing and doing: Visual supports for children with autism. *TEACHING Exceptional Children, 38*(6), 26–33.

Reed, P., & Gibson, E. (2005). The effect of concurrent task load on stimulus over-selectivity. *Journal of Autism and Developmental Disorders, 35,* 601–614.

Repp, A. C., Karsh, K. G., & Lenz, M. W. (1990). Discrimination training for persons with developmental disabilities: A comparison of the task demonstration model and the standard prompting hierarchy. *Journal of Applied Behavior Analysis, 23,* 43–52.

Schopler, E., Reichler, J., Bashford, A., Lansing, M., & Marcus, L. (1990). *Psycho-educational profile revised.* Austin, TX: Pro-Ed.

Originally published in *TEACHING Exceptional Children,* Vol. 41, No. 4, pp. 6–14.

# 4

# Teaching and Learning Approaches for Children With Asperger's Syndrome: Literacy Implications and Applications

*Francine Falk-Ross, Mary Iverson, and Carol Gilbert*

Asperger's syndrome (AS) is a grouping of physical and behavioral character-istics that introduces educational challenges for students of all ages, especial-ly at middle school levels when literacy activities involve inferential and critical levels of analysis. Often overlooked or misdiagnosed in primary level classrooms because the syndrome is still relatively unfamiliar to educators, the symptoms are not readily recognized by individual specialists, and the sub-tleties of behavior are often misleading. Several medical and special education researchers have re-introduced this social communicative disorder (e.g., Frith, 1991; Gillberg, 1995; Klin, Volkmar, & Sparrow, 2000; Twachtman-Cullen, 1996), describing the syndrome and its general characteristics in broad terms. Due to the increased awareness on the part of special education staff, students in private and public school systems have been identified in larger numbers. Because these students often remain in general education classrooms for var-ious lengths of time, it is beneficial for educators to become familiar with the specific idiosyncrasies of individuals with AS, their practical language sys-tems, and effective educational strategies.

To guide new learning, case studies extend people's understanding through naturalistic, psychological generalizations. Advantages of case stud-ies include application of theory to practice, activation of problem-solving skills, and immersion in authentic and relevant experiences (Elksnin, 1998); therefore, we chose a case study focus to describe students' discourse pat-terns, their educators' contextualization (or facilitation) cues, and the collab-orative intervention approaches characteristic of the two programs (i.e., one

*The authors are conversing about their students.*

clinically based and one school-based), for two children with Asperger's syndrome.

This article reviews descriptors of Asperger's syndrome, presents case studies, and addresses two lines of inquiry:

1. How do the characteristics of Asperger's syndrome manifest themselves in middle school children's language and literacy behaviors?
2. What forms of special education intervention and classroom accommodations will support these students' inclusion and achievement in general education classes?

We present individual manifestations of the disorder, familiarize teachers with beneficial compensatory educational strategies to use in the classroom, and target the practical application of theory into practice. The strategies described are for everyday use with children with AS in the middle grades (5-8), with attention to areas that are not routinely targeted, such as sensory processing, pragmatic strategies, and parent–teacher communication.

## CHARACTERISTICS OF ASPERGER'S SYNDROME

The cluster of symptoms referred to as Asperger's syndrome were first identified by Hans Asperger in 1944 at about the same time that Leo Kanner described the combination of behaviors now commonly referred to as autism. Asperger's syndrome was first included in the Diagnostic and Statistical Manual of Mental Disorders (DSM-IV) in 1994. Along with official recognition and additional research, the characteristics of this subcategory of pervasive developmental disorder (PDD) have been used to describe children with specific social communication difficulties. Researchers agree that there are variations among individuals displaying the characteristics of Asperger's syndrome in perceived intellectual abilities, sensory functioning, social skills, and gross motor development.

The DSM-IV (1994) described Asperger's syndrome as one of several pervasive developmental disorders. There is overlap among the disorders that compose the PDD classification, such as

- Obsessive–compulsive disorder (OCD).
- Nonverbal learning disability (NLD).
- Attention deficit and hyperactivity disorder (ADHD).
- Tourette syndrome.
- High-functioning autism (HFA).
- Retts syndrome.
- Hyperlexia.
- Pervasive developmental disorder not otherwise specified (PDD-NOS).

Similar to autism in that the salient characteristics are significantly impaired social–communicative interaction, noticeable perseverative–compulsive behavior, and delayed or disordered language development, symptoms of Asperger's syndrome differ in the subtlety and severity of various characteristics, and in some cases the presence of additional symptoms. For example, children with Asperger's syndrome usually have proficient verbal skills but have major difficulties responding to questions at inferential or critical levels. In specific social situations, they often interact inappropriately. In addition, these students typically have an IQ within the normal or above-normal range, but behavior problems such as inattentiveness, outbursts, anxiety, and low achievement levels negatively affect teacher perceptions. Students with Asperger's syndrome may also exhibit maladaptive behaviors that are mistakenly attributed to being willful or manipulative, when, in fact, these problems derive from difficulty understanding social interactions that often lead to inappropriate educational placements.

Unlike children who exhibit classic symptoms of autism, children with Asperger's syndrome are often misdiagnosed or undiagnosed for several years, delaying the help and support that they require. Research has suggested that the syndrome may be attributed to neurobiological dysfunction (Schultz, Romanski, & Tsatsanis, 2000; Wetherby & Prizant, 2000) or genetic factors (Gillberg, 1998).

## COMPENSATORY STRATEGIES RELATED TO SENSORY OVERSTIMULATION

Researchers have suggested the need for compensatory actions on the part of the teachers for addressing their reactions to students' sensory overstimulation in the classroom (Attwood, 1998; Myles, Cook, Miller, Rinner, & Robbins, 2000). In attempts to sustain or stabilize the sensitivities, students may

> **Intervention Strategies**
>
> To support students' communicative competence and educational achievement in the classroom, we targeted four areas of strategy development for this study.
>
> - First, we used compensatory strategies to decrease sensory over-stimulation during everyday educational activities.
> - Second, we introduced social skills strategies to enable students to engage in relational interactions with peers.
> - Third, we established language, literacy, and educational strategies to help provide independent problem-solving in discourse participation and curricular activities.
> - Last, we coordinated collaborative strategies between school specialists, teachers, and parents so that supportive emotional environments were available.

respond with avoidance behaviors in the classroom. Myles et al. (2000), described sensory overload as occurring in eight areas:

1. Smell
2. Movement
3. Balance
4. Muscular feedback
5. Taste
6. Hearing
7. Vision
8. Oral

They explain that ineffective sensory processing can create hyper- or hyposensitivities that distract children from completing tasks. Problems with over-sensitivity affect children's everyday experiences, such as brushing teeth, riding bikes, and tolerating their clothing. The strength of these physical reactions and the origin of the response (i.e., a student's neurological make-up) is what often separates children having Asperger's syndrome from children without the syndrome. Further examples from our experiences help to better define and understand how these problems manifest themselves in everyday experiences (Falk-Ross, Iverson, & Gilbert, 1997).

Strategies to help students with AS cope with these sensitivities might include visual cues. For example, black and white pictures or printed words to explain (or re-explain) directions would be helpful if they were attached to something readily available to the student, like a binder. Tactile cueing, such as a light tap on the shoulder, stimulates the student with AS to reorganize and pay attention to surrounding activities. Presentation of helpful auditory cues can also be used effectively.

In group settings, a "clicker" may be used by a teacher or a student. The teacher discusses the time and place for clicker use and usually places the rules on the board or on paper to provide visual cues. One instance when clicker use is appropriate is when topic maintenance is not sustained. The student or teacher may employ the clicker to draw attention to the loss of topic. When appropriate, a finger snap, throat clearing, or toe tapping are used.

To increase the organization of sensory information for students with AS, teachers can employ manipulatives (e.g., "worry stones") and weight-bearing activities (e.g., carrying heavy loads) that follow specific sensory requirements. These suggestions, referred to as a student's "sensory diet," are specific to each child and provide necessary sensory feedback. Implementation of oral motor activities appropriate to the treatment address oral sensitivities and feedback organization. For example, the speech and language pathologist may suggest helpful techniques, such as

- Variations in thermal stimulation (such as applying Popsicles and stroking the tongue and inside the mouth).
- Soft brushing movements (such as using small texturized instruments or NUK brushes).
- Oral resistive activities (such as chewing gum or hard pretzels).

Softening or changing the classroom lighting or using various colored transparencies or overlays affect visual sensitivities. Auditory sensitivity may be addressed by the reduction of noises, such as the ticking of the clock or someone tapping a pen or pencil.

Computer programs for memory activities, word finding, sequencing, transitioning to new topics; video and audio taping; and video reviews can increase auditory processing. These activities can help students compensate for sensory difficulties and can be integrated into everyday classroom activities by paraprofessionals as well as teachers and specialists (Falk-Ross, Iverson, & Gilbert, 1997).

## SOCIAL STRATEGIES FOR INTERVENTION

Children need to learn how to handle life experiences. Children with Asperger's syndrome often misinterpret the actions and discourse of others and need to learn communicative skills so that they have a better understanding of people. In terms of social communication, educators may teach pragmatic language through direct modeling for turn-taking—for example, through card games. Games address initiation of communication, response initiation, and topic maintenance. During the game, educators should address body language, facial cues, and gestures, along with recognition and interpretation of voice qualities during social skill groups. The reading or composing of personal social stories (Gray, 1994b) and writing them teaches children how to respond to social situations. Comic strip conversations (Gray, 1994a) are valuable tools

*One of the most important implications is that language and learning specialists and teachers need to identify and diagnose the presence of Asperger's syndrome in children at the earliest possible time.*

for visually showing the art of communication as well as demonstrating the emotions that people may exhibit. Having children act as a reporter for a local news center is a wonderful activity because it requires preparation, practice, and review of gestures, vocal tone, and intonation. Scripted storytelling through turn-taking between the student and the therapist is also an effective modeling and reading activity. Video-taping classroom activities such as these provide evidence for teachers to examine how effectively students communicate in the classroom using these activities.

Specific activities may help students in their social interactions within educational activities. For example, give the student with AS an explicit orientation to the school facilities to decrease the anxiety regarding transitioning. Introducing new teachers and aides is paramount to ensure familiarity for a child new to the particular environment. Meetings with staff members who regulate and structure extracurricular activities (such as lunch room interaction) help these students learn important rules for negotiating appropriate social and interaction strategies.

## BUILDING LANGUAGE AND EDUCATIONAL ACHIEVEMENT

Within classroom settings, various language routines, or forms of pedagogic discourse, accompany curricular activities (Cazden, 1998; Wells, 1998). Language routines lend predictability and organization to lessons in the forms of conversation and instruction in curriculum and clarification and correction of misunderstandings. The strong ties between language and education (Lemke, 1988; Nystrand, Gamoran, Kachur, & Prendergast, 1998; Tharp & Gallimore, 1988), and the premise that language and learning are socially constructed processes (Vygotsky, 1978; Wells & Chang-Wells, 1992) suggest the disadvantage that students with sociocommunicative disorders may experience without additional guided assistance. Examples of anticipated problems are in the realm of language use and discourse and educational tasks, such as summarizing and relating (i.e., comparing and contrasting), which become more abstract as children grow older and the problems associated with AS manifest themselves more frequently. In this case, a teacher would need to incorporate the use of visual organizers to provide a more concrete representation of the abstract information.

Difficulties with abstraction, a characteristic symptom of Asperger's syndrome, affect reading and writing achievement. Students' reading competencies are strongest in the areas of rule-governed language skills. For example, word identification strategies are mostly dependent on rigid graphophonic knowledge, strong sight word identification skills, and careful morphemic analysis. Contextual clues may help when they provide specific ties to the problem word (e.g., *gruff* and *bark* provide clues for *dog* in, "He heard the gruff bark of the dog."). Students' vocabulary knowledge is limited because multiple meanings are confusing, idioms are misunderstood, and definitions are memorized. In this case, teachers can have children illustrate the literal versus the intended meaning of the word (e.g., "It's raining cats and dogs").

In the area of reading comprehension, many literacy constructions are based on factual information; distractions and abstractions limit comprehension. For example, a student with AS easily understands literal-level questions and responds most exactly and appropriately. This student answers inferential questions with explicit reasoning and may offer alternative interpretations. Critical questions involving connections with the author's perspective, consideration of a different character's viewpoint, or ethics of a solution require social reasoning and are difficult to answer. Students with AS base their decisions concerning conclusions and implications on literal and rule-governed reasoning.

## COLLABORATIVE STRATEGIES AMONG SCHOOL SPECIALISTS, TEACHERS, PARENTS, AND ADMINISTRATORS

Students with AS need communication and support. If a student is receiving special education services, then the special education team is required to meet with the parents and the general education teachers who interact with the child. The nature of this meeting would be determined by the decisions made at the initial multidisciplinary meeting, often referred to as a *domain meeting* in which areas to be evaluated are determined. The results of the evaluations are discussed and the decisions relating to eligibility are determined at the

## Sample Case Studies

To understand how these characteristics of Asperger's syndrome develop with students' maturation, specific profiles are helpful. Although these specific behaviors are not mirrored in all students with this disorder, they represent some of the symptoms that occur and some of the problems they create for parents and teachers. Teachers may use this information to construct their own proposed solutions for their specific educational environments.

Two students who exhibited symptoms of Asperger's syndrome were studied for 1 school year. The students were enrolled in a variety of placements, including suburban public schools and a private after-school clinic where they received additional language remediation. The students participated in inclusive classrooms, where they received pull-out (resource) special education services. In addition to speech and language support, both students received occupational therapy, psychological and psychiatric counseling, social services, and behavioral therapy. Both students took prescribed medications and received primary language services from two speech and language pathologists—one served as teacher–researcher during this study. A speech and language pathologist initially evaluated the students for language delays or disorders, oral-motor deficits, and pragmatic communication strategies, and members of a special education team screened them for fine and gross motor skills and perceptual abilities.

The students received speech and language therapy services ranging from 2 to 5 hours per week during which new communication strategies were introduced. Strategy develop-ment was individualized, varying as necessary for appropriate educational achievement within the existing school curriculum. Common goals for each student, in addition to other individual goals, included

- Sensory integration instruction.
- Compensatory strategies for language use.

- Remedial work for auditory and visual processing deficits.

The names of the students have been changed, but the stories of their difficulties and competencies, typical of children with this syndrome in middle schools, are intended to assist teachers in identifying and addressing language problems related to Asperger's syndrome.

### Simon *(summarized from his mother's perspective)*

By the time Simon entered the first grade, he was a boy who seemed like he lived in a little black box, closed in from any outside stimuli. He didn't talk much and didn't want to talk about school. When I asked, "How was school? What did you do today?" he would respond angrily, "You asked me two questions at once and didn't even give me time to answer the first one!" I would then ask him only one question, wait for about a minute, and still not receive any response. In short, Simon would act as though he were a million miles away in his own world. This isolated, egocentric attitude continued through the middle school grades, and is a typical characteristic of students with AS.

At about this time, I noticed that he listened to certain CDs and watched a few movies repetitively, even more frequently than had occurred with my other two older children. One night he began naming every song on one of these CDs (it was "Miss Saigon") and what number each song was without looking at the CD! He became obsessed with listening to the death scene and at this point, I hid it so he could no longer listen to it. Another CD took its place as his obsession. Simon drew a picture of a mountain with spikes on one side and a slide down the other, repeatedly. He had to eat the same food every day and hated change of any kind. This repetitive nature of specific activities is another characteristic exhibited by students with AS

*continues*

### Sample Case Studies - *Continued*

and is observed in the home and at school by teachers.

Much of the time in elementary school, he cried. When I took him to school to wait on the playground until the bell rang, he would not get out of the car unless he could be close to me. We began to notice that his anxiety grew when he was in a crowd of people [that was] acting in a random fashion.

At school, Simon received special education services [for] his speech and language, learning disabilities, and social interaction. Outside of school, he received services from psychologists who understood both Simon and our family's situation, and we all began to come to terms with the realization that we needed to learn more about how to help our son.

It was not until the fifth grade that it was suggested to us by our therapists that Simon's varied characteristics were symptoms of Asperger's syndrome. When we first viewed the *Diagnostic and Statistical Manual of Mental Disorders,* Simon's odd characteristics fit this description. Specifically, he had a narrowed, intense focus on certain topics; a pedantic manner of speech and monotone; a lack of involvement with other children; a disregard for the reactions, interest, or—at times—feelings of others; and a lack of coordination in running, climbing, and use of stairs. Alone, any one of these characteristics would not cause concern, but the combination of these mirrored Asperger's syndrome.

Simon stayed in the local public school through the fifth grade. It was an experience fraught with frustration by family members, Simon, and his teachers. His teachers recognized his intelligence but could not seem to tap into it. As a team, [we] decided to place him in a communications development program in a different school instead of the local middle school. This alternative placement was staffed by a special education teacher, a speech and language teacher, a social worker, a vocational teacher, and an art therapist and had 10 other students. It was an environment that seemed more conducive to his progress and success. He began to learn and thrive there. He was taught how to relate to others, explored possible career choices through a vocational program, tried different classes outside of his program, and worked on coping with stress and anxiety in a variety of situations.

At one point during the year, he was doing so well in reading that his special education teacher felt he should try going into a general education reading class. Unfortunately, this did not prove to be a successful trial for Simon. While it became quickly apparent to family members that the material was much too difficult for him, his teachers steadfastly felt that he could do the work if he only tried harder. The reading material, which was on his grade level, had much more complicated plot lines, were much more interpretive, and required a much higher level of inferential thinking. When assigned to read the story during the reading period, he complained that his eyes were "sleepy" and he couldn't concentrate. His teachers misinterpreted this behavior as Simon "wasting time." When he arrived home, his tutor had to read the entire story with him and interpret and explain a great deal of it. He became confused and anxious.

Students with AS have a great deal of difficulty with understanding inferential or abstract meaning, often "shutting down" and requiring individual support. At this time it is important for teachers to reduce the pressure of the situation and wait out or talk through the problem with the [student with AS]. Teachers may misinterpret the behaviors due to the student's high functioning with literal material; in fact, teachers are often blinded by the student's strengths (Twachtman-Cullen, 1996). To this day, Simon's reading material consists of video game magazines, science fiction, and humor based on puns and political commentary.

*continues*

## Sample Case Studies - *Continued*

We have worked very hard with and for Simon. To say we have all learned a lot over the years would be a gross understatement. We have become entranced and fascinated with the complexities of the way Simon's brain works, and we certainly are much more familiar with how he reacts to situations. He has learned so much and accomplished so much more than has been expected of him. All we can say at this point is that his future is unknown, as it is for every child.

*Casey* (*as summarized by his speech and language pathologist*)

Casey had always been described as an extremely bright young student. The majority of his developmental milestones were reported to be within normal limits. His mother reported a history of early ear infections, and a speech delay was documented at 18 months. At approximately age 3, a note in the medical record appeared [that] suggested a diagnosis of Asperger's syndrome. This label afforded Casey appropriate educational and physical intervention at a young age through area health agencies.

I was able to observe Casey from his early elementary years through middle school. Casey was seen by the occupational therapist and treated by the school speech therapist for an articulation disorder. During his speech and language therapy sessions, recommendations for strategies to address the oral sensitivities and pragmatic issues were integrated into his educational program through private clinic work. Academically, Casey was always at or above age level in literacy achievement activities, but this was due to his spending many hours, sometimes 4 to 5 hours a night, on homework. This is typical of most students with Asperger's syndrome because of the obsessive–compulsive nature of their disorder and, and, as a result, their personalities.

Many aspects of the middle school environment became a source of stress and frustration for Casey and his teachers. The two main reasons for this frustration were the demands on socialization and the lack of rule-based movement. Recess, lunch, passing in the hall, and open physical education classes were all extremely difficult for Casey because of the often random nature of the required behavior.

A constant source of our conversations was the fact that he had no friends. Most of his peers teased and mocked his behavior. He had found a few friends that enjoyed the same structured activities that he did—for example, *Star Wars* games, Pokeman, and anything on the computer. The structure of computer games and programmed activities allowed for strictly linear thinking that is typical of students with this disorder. Because Casey had difficulty allowing others into conversations, most junior high students were not tolerant of his differences and would ignore him. This would have an impact on his participation in literacy activities that required interpretive response. Those friends toward whom he would gravitate were also interested in these same memory-heavy, organizationally rich activities. It was safe for Casey to remain immersed in his books or computers during the school day.

This further explains why Casey's need for interaction in the lunchroom and recess time outside were very sore subjects for Casey. He continually denied that junior high students were allowed out of the school during the day. He would emphatically state that there was not a recess time, although his denial was unfounded. He would do everything in his power to not go outside into those situations that were so difficult for him. At the lunch table to which he was assigned, the other students were social among themselves, but not with Casey. He usually ate quietly [and sat] apart at the table.

*continues*

**Sample Case Studies - *Continued***

On a few occasions, Casey was invited to participate in one of several "lunch groups" specially organized by the school's social worker, but these groups were difficult situations for him. These group activities were difficult due to [students with AS experiencing] problems with transitioning and with sharing perspectives (often referred to as "theory of mind").

Much of the work we did together focused on language and literacy support, using oral motor treatment. Many times movement was added, either on a swing or a large ball. This helped to improve jaw stability and improved Casey's ability to attend and organize. Through videotape feedback activities, Casey learned to identify difficulties in his handling of social situations (i.e., what went wrong and how he could alter reactions in different situations to have a more positive outcome).

After viewing our tape, Casey stated, "You know Mary, I could talk about computers all day. I have to remind myself to stop!" This remark was a reminder of the common problem that AS students share; they need to learn to self-cue for reactions from listeners in social situations. Recognizing the elements in social situations that need to be addressed is crucial to change. Role-playing has been an effective way to integrate specific lessons into life situations. Rehearsal or drill is also a means to improve skills necessary for efficient interaction.

One of the most difficult aspects of this treatment is finding someone to be a part of the sessions. Ignorance of the nature of the challenges and access to social partners for instructional classes are the limiting factors in the appropriate treatment of many of the areas of Asperger's syndrome. Appropriate use of pragmatic (i.e., social) language is a constant source of difficulty for students with Asperger's syndrome.

Casey has spent much of his time learning about his neurological system and how it functions. Literacy has been a haven and a means of learning. He was initially enrolled in the public school with speech and language support. Test scores and academic performance put Casey in the gifted range, and [he] is currently enrolled in a gifted school that addresses his social and pragmatic issues. He was monitored by staff and parents to ensure interactions with peers. Many of Casey's peers had similar interests, and there was more of a chance to communicate. The fact that Casey was able to maintain a public school educational placement was a tribute to his own hard work and the efforts of his family members who had worked so hard for this positive outcome.

*eligibility meeting.* All who will be working with the child are required to agree on how the child's goals and objectives will be addressed and what accommodations will be made to address the child's needs. Strategies are written into the individualized education program (IEP) that address the child's needs; for example, the child might need direct classroom support to reduce anxiety and to attend to language and social concerns. Educators and parents discuss questions regarding how anxiety is to be managed; how a crisis situation should be handled; how much homework should be assigned; and how the child's social and communicative needs will be addressed in the classroom, on the playground, and on the bus. The amount and kind of homework—if it is given—should be decided in very definite terms to prevent confusion for the parents at home.

## ADDRESSING HOMEWORK

In their book, *Asperger's Syndrome and Difficult Moments,* Myles and South-wick (1999) wrote that "the hours immediately following school are often the most difficult because the children are likely to be stress-filled and fatigued" (p. 97). One reason they gave for this difficulty is that the kids have had "to hold it together during school hours" (p. 97). Other roadblocks to the completion of homework are as follows:

• Difficulties with organizing materials and thoughts.
• Getting ideas down on paper.
• High distractibility.

For these reasons, homework can, and usually does, take much longer than expected. Myles and Southwick suggest providing a routine in which there is a regular study hour and place, with all materials on hand. Children with AS need to learn how to structure their homework, to decide on what homework should be completed first, and to learn how to follow a schedule with breaks built into it.

In *Asperger's Syndrome: A Guide for Educators and Parents,* Myles and Simpson (1998) suggested a home–school notebook for communication and assignments and recommend that teachers assign homework they are sure the parents can do. Parents should be prepared to re-explain and summarize material sent home and perhaps demonstrate what is to be done for that assignment. Some professionals believe that homework should not be assigned to AS students at all because of the stress put on the child and the resulting compromising of the home environment.

A parent's eyes provide an additional informative perspective to be valued. Different behaviors are seen at home compared to at school. Children with AS do not tend to relate or relive their experiences at school to family members. Still, parents can provide insight into areas of concern, such as subtle symbolic communication signals, relational problems with friends or educators, emotional overlays, and educational priorities. Their suggestions can guide teachers in how to handle situations that may impair the student's ability to function. Frequent feedback from parents and other family members is valuable.

## DISCUSSION AND IMPLICATIONS

Although all students who exhibit Asperger's syndrome display some degree of disorder in areas of behavioral functioning, the most salient characteristics for most students, including the two who were profiled, consist of

• The concreteness and narrow focus of language use and comprehension.
• The perseverative nature of language and physical behaviors.

- The awkward attempts at socialization and interaction with teachers and peers.
- The predisposition to sensory overload during curricular activities.

In general, these difficulties provided disruptions throughout the day, affecting the students' success, classroom routines, and teachers' frustrations.

Of the many remedial and compensatory educational strategies that were developed for each of the students, three general areas of instruction were most successful in supporting communicative competence and educational achievement. These include:

1. Decreasing sensory overstimulation.
2. Making educational accommodations.
3. Dealing with social skill problems.

Specifically, because of the rigid and concrete nature of language interpretation in students with Asperger's syndrome, teachers need to balance educational support strategies in the area of the humanities (reading, writing, social sciences) with scientific (math, science, technological) achievement potential. Classroom concerns must include a deeper consideration of variations in language routines, such as expansion of the typical initiation, response, and evaluation pattern (referred to as I.R.E.; Cazden, 1988) and tendencies toward sensory overload in our selective treatments of these children (Ayers, 1979).

One of the most important implications is that language and learning specialists and teachers need to identify and diagnose the presence of Asperger's syndrome in children at the earliest possible time. This means documenting all early childhood screenings, taking careful and detailed histories during parent interviews, and identifying the nature of social interaction (not just the quantity). Language and learning specialists need to be ready with teaching and learning strategies to help students with AS be successful. They need to be able to suggest and implement accommodations that adapt and modify curriculum requirements to suit these children's needs and sensitivities. This requires a more active role in teacher–specialist collaboration. Many schools are already assembling teams of specialists to collaborate for decision making regarding students with special needs.

Because students having symptoms of Asperger's syndrome are receiving placements in general education classrooms as part of mainstreaming or inclusion directives, sharing information about Asperger's syndrome and anecdotes of student profiles is beneficial to all school members.

# REFERENCES

American Psychiatric Association. (1994). *Diagnostic and statistical manual of mental disorders* (4th ed.). Washington, DC: Author.

Attwood, T. (1998). *Asperger's syndrome: A guide for parents & professionals.* Philadelphia: Jessica Kingsley.

Ayers, J. A. (1979). *Sensory integration and the child.* Los Angeles: Western Psychological Services.

Cazden, C. B. (1988). *Classroom discourse.* Portsmouth, NH: Heinemann.

Cazden, C. B. (1998, March). *Two meanings of "discourse."* Paper presented at the Annual Meeting of the American Association for Applied Linguistics, Seattle, WA.

Elksnin, L. K. (1998). Use of the case method of instruction in special education teacher preparation programs: A preliminary investigation. *Teacher Education and Special Education, 21*(2), 95–108.

Falk-Ross, F. C., Iverson, M. & Gilbert, C., (1997, May). *Teaching/Learning strategies for children with Asperger's syndrome.* Paper presentation at the Illinois Council for Exceptional Children, Spring Conference, Peoria, IL.

Falk-Ross, F. C., Iverson, M. & Gilbert, C., (2002). *Classroom-based language and literacy intervention: A problems and case studies approach.* Boston: Allyn & Bacon.

Frith, U. (1991). *Autism and Asperger's syndrome.* Cambridge, UK: Cambridge University Press.

Gillberg, C. (1995). Asperger's syndrome—Some epidemiological considerations: A research note. *Journal of Child Psychology and Psychiatry, 30,* 631–638.

Gillberg, C. (1998). Chromosomal disorders and autism. *Journal of Autism and Developmental Disorders, 28*(5), 415–425.

Gray, C. (1994a). *Comic strip conversations.* Arlington, TX: Future Horizons.

Gray, C. (1994b). *The social story book.* Arlington, TX: Future Horizons.

Klin, A. J., Volkmar, F. R., & Sparrow, S. S. (2000). *Asperger's syndrome.* New York, NY: Guilford.

Lemke, J. (1988). Genres, semantics, and classroom education. *Linguistics and Education, 1*(1), 81–90.

Myles, B. S., Cook, K. T., Miller, N. E., Rinner, L., & Robbins, L. A. (2000). *Asperger's syndrome and sensory issues: Practical solutions for making sense of the world.* Shawnee Mission, KS: Autism Asperger Publishing Company.

Myles, B. S., & Simpson, R. L. (1998). *Asperger's syndrome: A guide for educators and parents.* Austin, TX: PRO-ED.

Myles, B. S., & Southwick, J. (1999). *Asperger's syndrome and difficult moments: Practical solutions for tantrums, rage, and meltdowns.* Shawnee Mission, KS: Autism Asperger Publishing Company.

Nystrand, M., Gamoran, A., Kachur, R., & Prendergast, C. (1998). *Opening dialogue: Understanding the dynamics of language and learning in the English classroom.* New York: Teacher's College Press.

Schultz, R., Romanski, L., & Tsatsanis, K. (2000). Neurological modes of autistic disorders and Asperger's syndrome: Clues from neuroimaging (pp. 172–209). In A. Klin, F. Volkmar, & S. Sparrow (Eds.), *Asperger's syndrome.* (pp. 172–209.) New York, NY: Guilford Press.

Tharp, R. G., & Gallimore, R. (1988). *Rousing minds to life.* Cambridge, U.K.: Cambridge University Press.

Twachtman-Cullen, D. (1996). Blinded by their strengths: The topsy-turvy world of Asperger's syndrome. *The Advocate.* Autism Society of America Newsletter. Retrieved December 8, 2003, from http://www.udel.edu/bkirby/asperger/

Vygotsky, L. S. (1978). *Mind in society: The development of higher psychological processes.* Cambridge, MA: Harvard University Press.

Wells, G. (1998). Some questions about direct instruction—Why? To whom? How? And When? *Language Arts, 76*(1), 27–35.

Wells, G., & Chang-Wells, G. L. (1992). *Constructing knowledge together.* Portsmouth, NH: Heinemann.

Wetherby, A., & Prizant, B. (2000). *Autism spectrum disorders: A transactional developmental perspective.* Baltimore, MD: Brookes.

Originally published in *TEACHING Exceptional Children,* Vol. 36, No. 4, pp. 48–55.

# 5

# Facilitating Reading Comprehension for Students on the Autism Spectrum

*Susan E. Gately*

*Joshua is a 12-year-old student diagnosed with autism. He is very interested in the Civil War and knows many facts about the battles, uniforms, and weapons used, and he collects Civil War memorabilia. Although he is a voracious reader of this era, he has difficulty comprehending other topics during language arts class. Although he appears to understand story lines, he has difficulty understanding character motivation, perceiving foreshadowing, and appreciating event integration within a story. As a result, he avoids reading fiction and becomes easily frustrated with literature tasks.*

*Jamie is a second-grade student with a diagnosis of pervasive developmental delay (PDD). He has been a precocious decoder since preschool and is a fluent reader. He reads smoothly, often with appropriate prosody in his voice. It would seem that he understands what he is reading, but his fluency masks his lack of reading comprehension. Jamie thinks that reading stops with decoding and becomes visibly distressed when he is required to slow down and discuss what he reads.*

*Michelle is a fifth-grade student diagnosed on the autism spectrum. She attends school in a fifth-grade general education classroom and receives individualized and small group support with a special educator. She has difficulty understanding social situations but enjoys working with her small group. Her word recognition skills are almost at grade level and with assistance and individualized attention, she understands what she reads. However, when left on her own, she has trouble understanding even the lowest level material.*

Deficits in reading comprehension of children with autism spectrum disorder (ASD) are becoming increasingly highlighted in literature (Hale & Tager-Flusberg, 2005; Nation, Clarke, Wright, & Williams, 2006; O'Connor & Klein, 2004; Wahlberg, 2001). Smith-Myles et al. (2002) investigated the reading skills of children with Asperger's syndrome and found poorer silent reading skills than oral reading skills as well as significant differences between factual and higher order, inferential comprehension. Patterns of higher word reading skills accompanied by poor reading comprehension is often termed *hyperlexia*. The incidence of hyperlexia in the ASD population is increasingly being noted (Grigorenko, Klin, & Wolkmar, 2003; Newman et al., 2007).

It is a challenge for children with ASD to integrate language, social understanding, and emotional intent of messages to understand their social world (Quill, 2000). They often have deficits in language and social cognition and difficulty interpreting and labeling emotions and incorporating or integrating each of these aspects of communication to gain meaning in social situations. As in social situations, the task and importance of understanding and interpreting various cues is necessary for effective comprehension of narrative texts. To obtain reading comprehension, students must understand the author's vocabulary, style of writing, and story structure as well as characters' social experiences and how these contribute to the development of motivations, goals, and actions within a story setting. Students need to develop sensitivity to the emotions of characters and how these emotions play a role in characters' choices. Intuiting the motivation of characters and appreciating their intent are higher level comprehension skills which may be difficult for children with ASD.

Quill (2000) notes that "children with ASD tend to focus on details and interpret information in a fragmented manner; they misperceive the intentions of others and become 'stuck' in one mode of thinking and behaving" (p. 20). These characteristics predispose children with ASD toward difficulty understanding narrative text found in stories. Others speculate that the difficulty with narrative is in *theory of mind* (Sterling, 2002). Baron-Cohen (2001) suggests that theory of mind, the ability to infer the full range of mental states of others and the ability to reflect on one's own and other's actions, is a core deficit of ASD and often determines one's course of action. Baron-Cohen cites sources showing that children with ASD have difficulty understanding what others are thinking; understanding deception, metaphors, sarcasm, jokes, and irony; and developing one's imagination which may contribute to the difficulty with higher order understanding of narratives. Westby (2004) suggests that children with ASD often show deficits in theory of mind tasks which may result in difficulties in a variety of tasks regarding reading comprehension including (a) recognizing and understanding emotions, (b) incorporating pragmatic language skills, (c) determining character goals in stories, (d) recognizing false beliefs, and (e) understanding trickery. Even a simple fairy tale requires theory of mind skills, as most typical 4-year-olds will say, "Little Red Riding Hood *thinks* that it's her grandmother, but it's really the wolf" (Baron-Cohen). One can imagine

**Figure 1. Strategies for Higher Order Reading Comprehension Skills**

1. Priming background knowledge
2. Picture walks
3. Visual maps
4. Think-alouds and reciprocal thinking
5. Understanding narrative text structure
6. Goal structure mapping
7. Emotional thermometers
8. Social stories

the impact that deficits in theory of mind have on understanding more advanced stories.

## STRATEGIES FOR HIGHER ORDER READING COMPREHENSION SKILLS

There are a variety of strategies based on proficient reader research that can help children with ASD develop higher order reading comprehension skills and that can also be tailored to the cognitive characteristics of children with ASD. These strategies include priming background knowledge, picture walks, visual maps, think-alouds and reciprocal thinking, understanding narrative text structure, goal structure mapping, emotional thermometers, and social stories (see Figure 1). Incorporating visually cued instruction, such as graphics and color, with these strategies provides tangible and concrete information important for focusing on relevant parts of the story. Visually cued instruction also helps students remember what to do or say, decrease reliance on other prompts, and increase independence. As children become more automatic in responses, fade visual prompts.

Using a popular children's novel, *Sarah, Plain and Tall* (MacLachlan, 1985), helps demonstrate the strategies for higher order reading comprehension skills. This novel, routinely taught in fourth- and fifth-grade general education classrooms is part of interdisciplinary units within the United States. It is on many recommended reading lists and is included in curriculum frameworks in many states and school districts. Figure 2 provides a summary of the book.

### Priming Background Knowledge

Priming background knowledge, an important strategy to focus reading as a thinking activity, develops a mental set for an activity so that students connect what they know to new information and skills. Using tools such as picture walks and visual maps provides support to ensure that text is easier to

**Figure 2. Summary of *Sarah, Plain and Tall* (MacLachlan, 1985)**

Anna Whitting has taken care of her brother, Caleb, since her mother's death. She has also been responsible for the chores of their house on the prairie. Caleb, Anna, and their father, Jacob, continue to mourn the loss of their mother. Jacob puts an advertisement in the newspaper for a new wife. Sarah, a plain woman from Maine, answers the ad and prepares to move to the prairie.

understand. The more readers know about a topic, the easier it is to connect the text with background knowledge (Harvey & Goudvis, 2000). Although studies show that priming background knowledge is often helpful to children, they also indicate that when background knowledge is inaccurate, comprehension can be disrupted (Brody, 2001). And likewise, when children are given pertinent, accurate background knowledge, reading comprehension is enhanced (Brody). Many children with ASD have language deficits that result in a lack of general knowledge. This deficit has been shown to cause difficulty in accessing relevant knowledge and integrating it with what is in the text (Westby, 2004). As a result, while priming background knowledge, it is important that information be given that helps anchor thinking in the correct direction of the text.

## Picture Walks

To conduct a traditional picture walk, survey illustrations of a story, make predictions about the story, and confirm the predictions (Zimmerman & Hutchins, 2003). Engaging children in picture walks is an effective technique for struggling readers and helps children develop positive expectations about what might occur in a story. Prior to reading the story, review the pages of the book with the students while they think about the story and facilitate students' thinking by directing toward an accurate preview of the story. To ensure that incorrect assumptions are repaired and not reinforced while conducting picture walks with children with ASD, it is essential to maintain a more structured picture walk than may be needed for typically developing peers. Focusing children with ASD on pictures satisfies their tendency to learn visually and is more effective than simply talking or reading a summary of the book jacket. Beware that contradictory relationships between text and illustrations may occur (Serafini, 2004) and therefore care must be taken to select illustrations that enhance the text.

## Visual Maps

When there are no pictures to use to prime background knowledge, using visual maps to set up stories is an effective alternative. One type of visual map

**Figure 3. Visual Map for *Sarah, Plain and Tall***

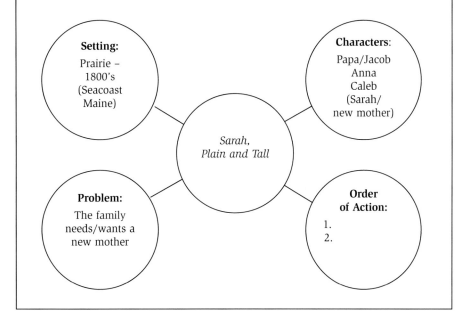

Prior to putting together a visual map, consider how much background information to give to students, the individual needs of the students, and what students
already know. Insert the title of the book in the middle and by collaborating with
students write in the setting and characters introduced at the beginning of the
story and add the problem to help the student appreciate the action. Add action
statements (order of action) as the problem is resolved. Add the information in
parentheses as the story progresses.

is a simple story map. This helps students get "primed" for what they will read
by giving information about characters, setting, and the problem faced by the
characters. As seen in Figure 3, include story elements that are introduced at
the beginning of *Sarah, Plain and Tall* in the beginning of the lesson. Enhance
the graphic as new details develop such as when Sarah is introduced into the
story, the characters enter a new setting (e.g., the seacoast of Maine), or the
characters engage in additional action sequences. Collaborate with the students as the visual map is developed. Enlarge the "order of action" bubble so
that students write down the action as it occurs in the story.

## Think-Alouds and Reciprocal Teaching

Think-alouds is another way to model thinking about text to students. Used in
reciprocal teaching (Palinscar & Brown, 1985), think-alouds help students
with disabilities learn four strategies: predicting, questioning, clarifying, and
summarizing. Think-alouds are recommended for children having difficulty

with the meta-cognitive aspects of reading (Reutzel & Cooter, 2001). Use think-alouds (Tovani, 2000) by carefully selecting a passage based on the strategy modeled. In reciprocal teaching, explicitly teach students the four strategies by modeling thinking through the story with the students. As the passage is read aloud, stop often to share thoughts, often the exact thought of that moment relating to the story. The shared thoughts should be explicit; that is, point out to the students the words that specifically trigger the thoughts. For example, "When I read the words XYZ, I thought about ABC" or "I'm confused about ABC. Let's see how I can figure this out." Explicit teaching helps students gradually assume responsibility for using the four strategies. Eventually, have students talk about their own thinking, answer direct questions, develop questions to ask other students, or make comments to share with group members. This mediated scaffolding is essential to help students become independent in their ability to understand text.

Westby (2004) notes that poor comprehenders do not build mental models and are less skilled at integrating information from different parts of text in order to make relevant inferences. The information processing deficits of children with ASD highlights their difficulty with integration and their tendency to over select and focus attention to one detail at a time (Quill, 2000). Adding color coding and using props adds visual cues that help students remember the four strategies as well as enhance overall instruction. Another way to provide visual cues to aid different ways to think about and make the text concrete is to write thoughts about the story on colored post-it notes.

## Understanding Narrative Text Structure

Understanding narrative text structure is another technique to help students improve comprehension skills and organize narrative text into a coherent whole. Basic understanding of narrative starts with discovering who the main character of the text is and what he did. Teaching basic actor words (e.g., man, woman, Jane, Bill, grandparents, dogs, and relatives) and basic action words (e.g., ate, jumped, cried, slept, and ran) and then combining the two words to make a complete thought helps develop text structure. Use simple sentences and pictures at the beginning of this instruction and eventually students learn to identify who-did-what as they are repeatedly asked questions such as, "Who ran?" or "What did the girl do?" When reading a simple story, develop a sequence of who-did-what events and have students list these events in simple story frames (see Figure 4). Events of the story can be written on sentence strips, organized by the students, and then matched to the cues in the story frame. Sequencing these events can be a subsequent activity and color coding the who-did-what frames adds a visual cue to help students develop the narrative text. As the skill of identifying the sequence of action by listing who-did-what is developed, students can be shown how to insert transitional words to help write series of who-did-what sentences by modifying the simple story frames (see Figure 5).

**Figure 4. Simple Who-Did-What Sequence**

| Who | Did What |
|---|---|
| 1. Anna's mother | died. |
| 2. Anna | takes care of family. |
| 3. Father | writes newspaper ad. |
| 4. Caleb | waits and hopes. |
| 5. Sarah | answers the ad. |

## Goal Structure Mapping

Once children understand the who-did-what structure and how a series of who-did-what-statements creates a narrative, introduce goal structure mapping. Developed by Sundbye (1998), goal structure mapping uses shapes, lines, and arrows to organize stories so that students understand how events of one character may influence the actions of another character. To prime students to use good structure mapping, in a modified form of goal structure mapping, introduce students to a basic graphic which depicts who-did-what. Add additional actions to the graphic showing who-did-what as the story develops. Once graphics for the goal and the resolution of the goal/story are added, the students may begin to use Sundbye's Goal Structure Mapping Program to follow the story line. Basic level visual maps are shown in Figure 6. From this frame, have students use simple color-coded organizers to develop a story summary which includes the character's goal, his actions to achieve that goal, and a conclusion noting if the character attained his goal.

Once students master how to understand the major events of the story, draw arrows to introduce the concept that one character's action may influence another character's action. A goal structure map for *Sarah, Plain*

**Figure 5. Transferred Data to Story Frame**

Give the story frame (in bold) to students to fill in with information transferred from the who-did-what phase (see Figure 4).

**This story is about** Caleb and Anna.

**First,** Anna's mother died.

**Then,** Anna take cares of her family.

**Next,** Father writes a newspaper ad.

**After that,** Caleb waits and hopes for a new mother.

**Finally,** Sarah answers the ad.

**I** liked the story.

**Figure 6. Goal Structure Mapping**

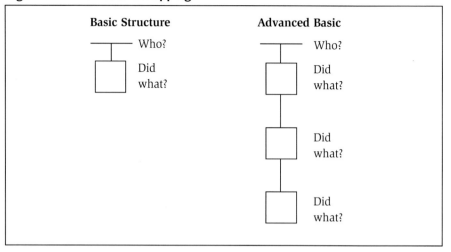

*and Tall* is developed with the students in a sequential fashion. It shows how the action of one character influences the action of another with arrows. This aspect of goal structure mapping is quite helpful to students with ASD because it not only shows the order of action but also helps the students to see the relationship of actions between the characters. It is another step toward helping students with ASD think about why characters do what they do. Sometimes they act because of another character's influence. This is often difficult for students with ASD to grasp. Although the final product may look complicated, it is developed with the student in a sequential fashion. Making goal structure maps for each chapter or sequence of events helps students keep the storyline organized.

## Emotional Thermometers

Helping students understand feelings and emotions of characters is important in enhancing student's appreciation of why characters make certain choices. Using emotional thermometers (Westby, 2004) with color and varied vocabulary helps children gain a sense of various intensities of feelings (see Figure 7). Gray (1994) suggests that color connotes emotions and can be used to help children with ASD understand and describe feelings and emotions for themselves as well as characters in stories. For example, she suggests that green connotes good ideas and happy feelings whereas red connotes bad ideas or angry feelings. Shades of color can be used to (a) help children "see" the intensity of feeling in a concrete manner, (b) identify characters' feelings, (c) show the difference between protagonists and antagonists, (d) show how characters' feelings may change with different events, (e) and show how feelings often affect characters' choices. Gray (1994) also uses colors in comic strip conversations which further differentiates characters' thoughts from actions by using cartoon bubbles (see Figures 8 and 9).

**Figure 7. Emotional Thermometer**

Using the color blue, direct students to point to varying shades to express the level of sadness that Papa is feeling.

## How sad was Papa after his wife died?

a little sad                              very sad

## Social Stories

Understanding characters' actions in reading requires understanding various thinking perspectives, which is often difficult for children with ASD. Gray (2003) uses social stories to help children consider perspectives of others in social situations and help consider perspectives of various characters. For example, a social story about Caleb's feelings in *Sarah, Plain and Tall* are analogized to a student's similar feelings in a different situation, helping the student gain a higher level of appreciation and understanding of the story.

> I am reading *Sarah, Plain and Tall.* It is a story about a family who lives on a prairie. Caleb is the little boy in the story. His mother died when he was born. Caleb misses his mother. I can tell this because Caleb keeps asking his sister Anna to tell him about his mother. When I think about Caleb missing his mother, I can think about missing my brother who is at college. I am sad when my brother

**Figure 8. Cartoon Bubbles**

Sometimes characters say one thing and may mean another. Use cartoon bubbles to help differentiate between what a character thinks and what a character says.

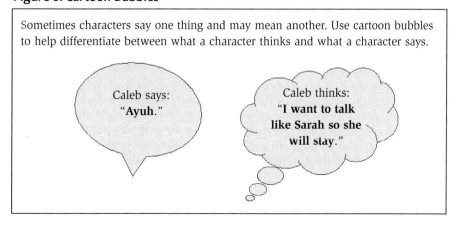

**Figure 9. Cartoon Bubbles in Comic Strips**

Develop comic strip conversations with students using crude drawings.
Use these comic strip conversations to help students understand characters'
emotions, feelings, and perspectives.

leaves for college. This helps me to know how Caleb feels in the
story.

Social stories can also help students understand language which may
seem contradictory to a character's actions.

When Sarah writes a letter to the family, Caleb reads the letter "so
many times that the ink begins to run and the folds tear." Caleb is
not trying to ruin the letter. He is very interested in the letter, so he
reads it over and over. Sometimes I get very excited about something
and I talk about it over and over. This is what Caleb is doing in the
story. This tells me that Caleb is very interested in Sarah and he is
hoping she will come to live with the family and be his mother.

Social stories help students understand text and may be used to help
reduce any difficulty using any of the strategies previously mentioned. In the
following social story, the student is directed to use the same strategies as his
classmates to help him understand what he reads.

When my classmates read *Sarah, Plain and Tall,* they look for clues
that help them understand how Caleb feels and what he wants. This
is a good idea. Sometimes they find the clues and sometimes they
can't find the clues. The teacher can help them understand about
Caleb. Sometimes I miss the clues too. This is ok. The teacher and
my classmates can help me understand about Caleb and the other
characters.

Social stories assist students to make important connections to characters that they otherwise might overlook or misinterpret. They can also be tailored to the individual child and the individual strategy that needs to be learned using the student's curriculum.

## CONCLUSION

For Joshua, Jamie, and Michelle many of the techniques discussed may be effective in assisting reading comprehension. Using shaded color strips to show varied states of emotion, social stories to connect character emotional states to personal experiences, and using thought bubbles to differentiate thoughts from actions may help Joshua facilitate understanding why characters take various actions in narrative text. Making predictions and reading to validate those predictions and teaching story structure with visuals and color may also improve Joshua's ability to anticipate the storyline.

For Jamie, who has difficulty focusing on reading as a meaningful activity, modeling strategies and developing a set procedure for reading may be an effective way to help him with reading comprehension. Jamie might be taught to first focus on who-did-what sequences in stories and gradually build graphics to think about character problems and potential solutions.

Although Michelle may also benefit from many of the strategies recommended in this article, she primarily needs assistance developing self-guided strategies for reading comprehension. Giving Michelle a color-coded system reminds her to look at pictures, make predictions, and focus on who-did-what sequences as she reads. Using goal structure mapping techniques may also give her the visual cueing system needed for reading comprehension. In addition, she may also profit from instruction that builds in scaffolding so that she is increasingly expected to respond to questions on her own.

Priming background knowledge, using think-alouds to develop strategies for understanding, learning story structure, and using comic strip bubbles and social stories enhanced by visual graphics and color help students with ASD anticipate action, follow narration, and think about character emotions and intent. The strategies are easy to implement and can be easily taught to general education teachers and paraprofessionals. Using these strategies with all students in the general education classroom will not only benefit students with ASD within general education classrooms, but can enhance the instruction of all students.

## REFERENCES

Baron-Cohen, S. (2001). Theory of mind and autism: A review. *Special issue of the International Review of Mental Retardation, 23*, 169–176.

Brody, S. (2001). *The Brody reading manual: An implementation guide for teachers* (2nd ed.) Milford, NH: Brody.

Gray, C. (1994). *Comic strip conversations.* Jenison Public Schools, MI: Future Horizons.

Gray, C. (2003). *Updated guidelines and criteria for writing social stories*™. Arlington, MI: Future Horizons.

Grigorenko, E. L., Klin, A., & Wolkmar, F. (2003). Annotation: Hyperlexia: Disability or superability? *Journal of Child Psychology and Psychiatry, 44*(8), 1079–1091.

Hale, C. M., & Tager-Flusberg, H. (2005). Social communication in children with autism: The relationship between theory of mind and discourse development. *Autism: The International Journal of Research and Practice, 9*(2), 157–178.

Harvey, S., & Goudvis, A. (2000). *Strategies that work.* York, ME: Stenhouse.

MacLachlan, P. (1985). *Sarah, plain and tall.* New York: Harper Collins Children's Press.

Nation, K., Clarke, P., Wright, B., & Williams, C. (2006). Patterns of reading ability in children with autism spectrum disorder. *Journal of Autism and Developmental Disorders, 36*(7), 911–919.

Newman, T. M., Macomber, D., Naples, A. J., Babitz, T., Volkmar, F., & Grigorenko, E. L. (2007). Hyperlexia in children with autism spectrum disorders. *Journal of Autism and Developmental Disorders, 37*(4), 760–774.

O'Connor, I. M., & Klein, P. D. (2004). Exploration of strategies for facilitating the reading comprehension of high-functioning children with autism spectrum disorders. *Journal of Autism and Developmental Disorders, 34*(2), 115–127.

Palincsar, A. S., & Brown, A. L. (1985). Reciprocal teaching: Activities to promote read(ing) with your mind. In T. L. Harris & E. J. Cooper (Eds.), *Reading, thinking and concept development: Strategies for the classroom.* New York: The College Board.

Quill, K. A. (2000). *Do-Watch-Listen-Say.* Baltimore: PHB.

Reutzel, D. R., & Cooter, R. B. (2001). *Strategies for reading assessment and instruction helping every child succeed* (2nd ed). New York: Pearson/Merrill.

Serafini, F. (2004). *Lessons in comprehension explicit instruction in the reading workshop.* Portsmouth, NH: Heinemann.

Smith-Myles, B., Hilgenfeld, T. D., Barnhill, G. P., Griswold, D. E., Hagiwara, T., & Simpson, R. L. (2002). Analysis of reading skills in individuals with Asperger syndrome. *Focus on Autism and Other Developmental Disabilities, 17*(1), 44–47.

Sterling, L. (2002). *Autism and theory of mind.* Retrieved January 6, 2005, from http://darkewing.uoregon.edu/ ~ sterling/

Sundbye, N. (1998). *Goal structure mapping.* Lawrence, KS: Curriculum Solutions.

Tovani, C. (2000). *I read it, but I don't get it: Comprehension strategies for adolescent readers.* Portland, ME: Stenhouse.

Wahlberg, T. J. (2001). *The ability to comprehend written text in high functional individuals with autism.* Unpublished doctoral dissertation, Northern Illinois University, Dekalb, IL.

Westby, C. (2004, April). *Reading between the lines for social and academic success.* Paper presented at 9th Annual Autism Spectrum Disorders Symposium, "Social and Academic Success for Students With ASD," Providence, RI.

Zimmerman, S., & Hutchins, C. (2003). *7 Keys to comprehension: How to help your kids read it and get it.* New York: Three Rivers Press.

Originally published in *TEACHING Exceptional Children,* Vol 40, No. 3, pp. 40–45.

# 6

# Mathematics Interventions for Students With High Functioning Autism/ Asperger's Syndrome

*Jeffrey B. Donaldson and Dianne Zager*

*Teachers are often at a loss when considering how to address mathematics difficulties for students with high functioning autism/Asperger's syndrome (HFA/AS). Students may show difficulty remembering operations throughout an equation, organizing information on the page, and comprehending the language in instructions or word problems (Minshew, Goldstein, Taylor & Siegel, 1994). These difficulties are, in fact, very similar to the mathematics impairments demonstrated by students with nonverbal learning disability (NLD), a right hemispheric neurological impairment which greatly affects the ability of students to succeed in mathematics (Rourke & Tsatsanis, 2000). Because NLD is defined neuropsychologically, mathematics interventions are more easily developed, and have proven effective (Rourke & Tsatsanis, 2000).*

Nonverbal learning disability (NLD) and autism are diagnostically separate entities. NLD is primarily defined through a neuropsychological profile, whereas identification of autism is accomplished through observational information (American Psychiatric Association, 2000). However, there are clear behavioral and cognitive similarities between NLD and high functioning autism/Asperger's syndrome (HFA/AS; Rourke & Tsatsanis, 2000). Recognition and appreciation of existing similarities among individuals in these two diagnostically distinct groups may prove helpful when developing instructional interventions.

NLD's neuropsychological definition as a right-hemispheric brain dysfunction provides some insight for targeting instruction. Because NLD and HFA share several prominent features (see Figure 1), it appears that in the area of mathematics, students with both disorders would benefit from similar planning and accommodation strategies (Rourke, Fisk, & Strang, 1986). Recommendations that fit the overarching patterns of cognitive deficits and strengths for NLD and HFA/AS are presented in this article. We utilized a literature review to form a theoretical foundation for evidence-based instructional practices that would engage students with both NLD and HFA/AS, including Integrated Behavioral Experiential Teaching (IBET; Zager, 2006).

## HFA/AS AND NLD

## HFA or AS?

In the current literature, there is a discussion of whether HFA and AS are the same disorder. A study by Klin, Volkmar, Sparrow, Cicchetti, & Rourke (1995) examined these groups with regard to neuropsychological characteristics, finding significant similarities and differences. Further study by Macintosh and Dissanayake found minimal qualitative differences between high functioning autism and Asperger's syndrome (Macintosh & Dissanayake, 2004), providing empirical evidence to support a unitary treatment of these disorders. For the purpose of this article, HFA and AS are combined and are referred to as HFA/AS.

**Figure 1. Behavioral and Neuropsychological Symptoms of HFA/AS, NLD**

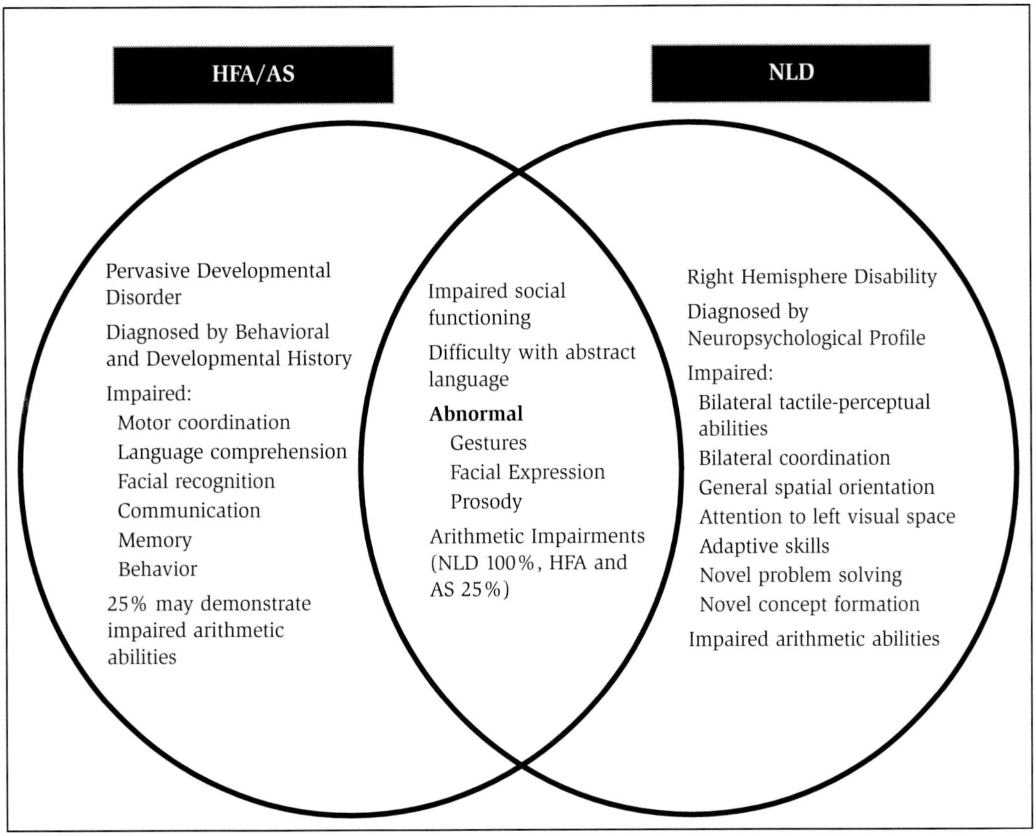

*Note.* AS = Asperger's syndrome. HFA = high functioning autism. NLD = nonverbal learning disability.

## Similarities of HFA/AS and NLD

Clinical features of HFA/AS and NLD reveal a similar pattern of behavior and adaptive functioning, particularly in impaired social functioning. Prosody, facial expression, gaze, gestures, and overall body language are sufficiently atypical to differentiate individuals in both groups from their neurotypical peers (Rourke & Tsatsanis, 2000). They tend to have difficulty understanding the social world and have problems utilizing interpersonal and group environments to meet their needs. Rourke and Tsatsanis also noted general interpersonal awkwardness apparent upon interaction.

## Deficits of HFA/AS: Communication and Social

Features of HFA/AS include marked deficits in several areas. According to Szatmari, Tuff, Finlayson, and Bartolucci (1990), communication of individuals on the spectrum is often pedantic, involving lengthy and one-sided dis-

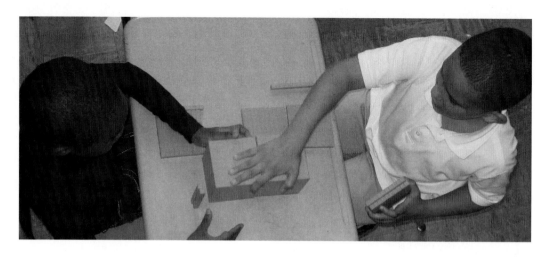

course. Appreciation of humor is limited, with overreliance on literal interpretation. Poor comprehension and application of nonverbal aspects of communication including facial expression, gestures, prosody, and a limited ability to understand and use the rules governing social behavior are also apparent. Problems with nonverbal communication are frequently reflected in difficulty maintaining reciprocal interaction and forming friendships.

## Deficits of HFA/AS: Mathematics

A student may exhibit impaired visuospatial abilities and motor skill deficits (Szatmari et al.,1990). Because mathematics requires visuospatial coordination, such impaired visuospatial abilities can lead to difficulties in math skill acquisition and frustration in related learning situations.

Popular culture often depicts persons with HFA/AS demonstrating high levels of mathematical ability, for example, in the movie *Rain Man* and in books such as *The Curious Incident of the Dog in the Night-time*. However, Williams, Goldstein, Kojkowski, and Minshew (2008) found that mathematics disability, defined by WISC-III arithmetic subtest scores at least one standard deviation less than vocabulary subtest scores, is demonstrated by at least 25% of students with HFA/AS.

These students may exhibit similar patterns of mathematical difficulties as students with NLD (described in the following), including such challenges as difficulty remembering operations throughout an equation, organizing information on the page, and comprehending the language in instructions or word problems (Minshew, Goldstein, Taylor & Siegel, 1994).

## Deficits of NLD: Mathematics

In NLD, right hemisphere language/information processing impairments include difficulty understanding metaphors, abstract language, sarcasm, and humor. Rourke and Strang (1978), after examining differences between students matched for mathematics difficulties but varying in their reading and spelling abilities, described the following patterns of mathematical errors in students: (a) calculations were attempted for which students had little understanding of task requirements; (b) there was a tendency to misread signs; (c) work was often disorganized, with faulty alignment of rows and columns and occasional omission of entire steps of calculation; (d) there was a general avoidance of unfamiliar arithmetic operations; (e) errors reflected the student's difficulty remembering arithmetic tables or steps in procedures. These difficulties were related to "basic problems in visuospatial organizational skills, psychomotor coordination, complex tactile-perceptual skills, reasoning, concept formation, mechanical arithmetic, and scientific reasoning" (Spreen, Risser, & Edgell, 1995, p. 489), all of which would substantially undermine a student's capacity to acquire new skills and concepts in mathematics.

Mathematics challenges of NLD, including difficulty with organizing work, trouble with steps in procedures, and a tendency to misread signs, require sustained conscious awareness on the part of the instructor, but are amenable to remediation using cognitive strategies (Rourke, 1989). Students with NLD also demonstrate impairment in visuospatial and mathematical abilities. Right hemisphere language impairments are exhibited, including trouble understanding metaphors, abstract language, sarcasm, and humor.

## Deficits of NLD: Neuropsychological

Neuropsychological deficits for students with NLD include bilateral tactile-perceptual, visuospatial and coordination difficulties, problems with novel problem solving and novel concept formation, and poor mechanical arithmetic. Students with NLD often have difficulty with their social perception and judgment (Rourke & Tsatsanis, 2000), and their interactions tend to be characterized by high levels of repetitive verbal conversation (Pelletier, Ahmad, & Rourke, 2001). Problems in adapting to novel situations are also documented (Rourke, 1989). These deficits, especially in comprehension of abstract information, may affect acquisition of fundamental mathematics concepts, including numeration, place value, and estimation (Bos & Vaughn, 2002).

## Evidence for a Unitary Treatment of HFA/AS and NLD

Williams et al. (2008) reported evidence to substantiate an overlap in math learning characteristics between the two groups. These researchers found that mathematics disability, which is one of the most prominent features of NLD, is shared by at least 25% of students with HFA/AS (defined by arithmetic subtest scores at least one standard deviation less than vocabulary subtest scores). Furthermore, at least one of the three primary components of the Wechsler pattern seen in NLD was found in 17% to 26% of the children and 20% to 32% of the adults with HFA (Williams et al., 2008). This documented overlap in mathematical impairment between the two groups provides support for similar treatment of the two populations.

Further review of the literature provides support for associating characteristics of NLD to HFA/AS. Joseph, Tager-Flusberg, and Lord (2002) reported that students with autism spectrum disorders (ASD) generally presented with uneven cognitive development, with some students presenting with higher verbal skills and lower nonverbal skills (e.g., mathematics). In addition, a study by Mayes and Calhoun (2003) found that on achievement tests, students with HFA/AS were found to present with lower WISC-III scores in the domain of arithmetic. Another study by Mayes and Calhoun (2005) found that 67% of students with autism also exhibited learning disabilities. Goldstein, Beers, Siegel, and Minshew (2001) described how the students with HFA who most resembled students with NLD were those who showed better achievement in reading than in math. These findings indicate that a significant portion of students with HFA/AS demonstrate similar mathematics difficulties as students with NLD. It is important that educators incorporate this information into instructional programming.

## INSTRUCTIONAL STRATEGIES

The following recommendations have been made for treating students with learning disabilities in mathematics. In light of the documented overlap between HFA/AS and NLD (e.g., Joseph et al., 2002; Williams et al., 2008), the recommendations should also prove helpful to students with HFA who exhibit mathematical difficulties. Miller, Butler, and Lee (1998) identified several practices that have been demonstrated effective for students with learning disabilities. From these practices, four have been selected by the authors as

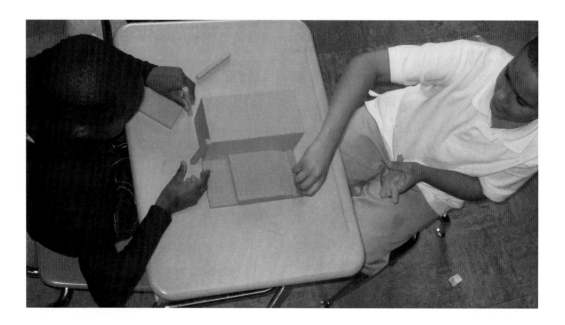

particularly well suited for students demonstrating the constellation of deficits described earlier. A fifth strategy, Integrated Behavioral Experiential Teaching (IBET) has been included, as it has been developed specifically for the needs of the HFA/AS population in mathematics.

One strategy that has been used in math instruction for students with learning differences is *self-regulation*. Self-regulation involves students completing checklists as they perform computations, with reminders for each step; teacher feedback follows completion of the tasks. In the realm of computation, Dunlap & Dunlap (1989) found that, with self-regulation, student solution accuracy increased as their mood became more positive. Verbal feedback strategies, in which students are asked to repeat salient directions that will strengthen the concepts, help create structure, and ensure that the student comprehends each step (Spreen et al., 1995).

A second strategy is *direct instruction*, the use of systematic instruction that demonstrates how to perform tasks, prompts and guides the learner, and reinforces correct responses. Direct instruction relies on curriculum-based assessment to identify specific skills to teach. Accurate responses are rewarded; inaccurate responses are redirected, with an emphasis on students learning strategies for computation or problem solving. Utilizing a direct instruction intervention for computation, Van Houten and Rolider (1990) taught students to match a numeral to a specific color to teach number names, with two thirds of the subjects tested demonstrating 100% accuracy 4 months posttest. In another direct instruction intervention for problem solving, Wilson and Sindelar (1991) successfully taught addition and subtraction word problems to students with learning disabilities. Students receiving this direct instruction performed significantly better than the control group.

*Goal structure* utilizes goal setting and contingent rewards for completion of mathematics tasks. Fuchs, Bahr, and Rieth (1989) used goal setting to assist in teaching computation and found that students demonstrated some improvement after setting personal goals for themselves, knowing that rewards were in store for strong performance. As noted by Miller et al. (1998), the students often set the same targets for themselves as the reviewers estimated, indicating that the students had an internal representation of what strong performance meant.

Yet another strategy, *concrete-representational-abstract* (CRA), has been used to teach fractions. In CRA, students are first shown concrete examples (two halves of an apple), then they might be shown a representation (a picture of two halves of a square), followed by the abstract depiction of the concept (the fraction ½). In studying computation problems, Miller and Mercer (1993b) found that students learning about money and unit conversions achieved 80% mastery for concepts taught after five 20-minute lessons at each stage. In problem solving, Miller and Mercer (1993a) determined that students who learned word problems, having had no exposure to word problems previously, when taught using a concrete-representational-abstract sequence, performed at a mean level of 87%. A multisensory model that uti-

> **Additional Resources**
>
> Byron Rourke is a preeminent researcher in the field of NLD. His web site is http://www.nld-bprourke.ca/
>
> Further developments in the fields of Education and Neuropsychology can be found at http://scholar.google.com/
>
> Resources for special education teachers may be found at the National Association of Special Education Teachers, http://www.naset.org/

lizes concrete-to-representational-to-abstract sequence of instruction has been demonstrated to be effective for teaching algebra (Witzel, 2005). Because students with HFA/AS or NLD are challenged in their processing of abstract concepts (Rourke & Strang, 1978), CRA is a useful model of instruction for these students.

Finally, *Integrated Behavioral Experiential Teaching* (IBET) is an approach that has been used to teach children with ASD fundamental academic and social skills (Zager, 2006). IBET uses elements of direct instruction in its use of behavioral principles and CRA in its emphasis on concrete presentation of stimuli first (often through real-life experiences, then a transition to photographic representations, followed by abstract symbols) to integrate skills in order to create a vivid concrete experience for the student. IBET utilizes students' direct personal experiences to make learning salient through photographs and experiential learning in combination with errorless learning and systematic reinforcement. The learning is not only visual, but also involves embedding multisensory prompts and cues directly in the instructional stimuli (Zager, 2007; Zager & Gattasse, 2004).

The strategies presented in Figure 2 apply to students with nonverbal learning disabilities and those students with HFA who demonstrate mathematical difficulties. Figure 2 relates instructional objectives to strategies to help guide educators in teaching students to overcome math difficulties.

## CONCLUSION

If a teacher has a student with HFA/AS in his or her classroom, there is a one in four chance that student will demonstrate difficulties with mathematics. Because of the overlap between individuals with NLD and HFA, their demonstrated commonalities can be used to inform teachers' practice in lesson planning, differentiation, assessment, and grouping of students with HFA/AS.

Depending on the difficulties the student demonstrates, a teacher may select interventions or strategies geared toward the specific age, instructional needs, and motivation of the individual student. If an older student becomes frustrated easily when working on mathematics and has difficulty organizing

**Figure 2. Instructional Objectives and Corresponding Strategies for Instruction**

| Important Skills for Success in Mathematics (Novick & Arnold, 1988; Rourke, & Strang, 1978) | Strategies to Develop Mathematics Skills for Students With HFA/AS and NLD |
|---|---|
| Students will develop adequate discrimination skills to differentiate between multiple inputs and provide the appropriate response. | IBET |
| Students will develop the ability to maintain one-to-one correspondence between object and number. | IBET |
| Students will be able to shift between visual (block) and verbal (number label) modalities. | IBET, CRA |
| Students, in order to maintain a steady work pattern, will develop the ability to remain on task for the appropriate amount of time, maintaining an effective level of engagement. | Goal Structure, IBET, Self-Regulation |
| Students will demonstrate age- and grade-appropriate numeration skills, including numbers, and their quantities. | IBET, Direct Instruction |
| Students will demonstrate age- and grade-appropriate skills in assigning place value. | IBET, Self-Regulation, CRA |
| Students will understand the requirements of a math problem before they begin the solution. | Self-Regulation |
| Students will read signs correctly. | Direct Instruction, IBET |
| Students will display appropriately organized work, with numbers aligned into columns. | Self-Regulation, Direct Instruction |
| Students will demonstrate appropriate use of arithmetic tables. | Self-Regulation |
| Students will perform every step of the calculations. | Self-Regulation, Direct Instruction |
| Students will apply prior knowledge to unfamiliar or novel operations. | IBET, Direct Instruction |
| Students will demonstrate age- and grade-appropriate skills in estimation. | IBET, CRA |

*Note.* AS = Asperger's syndrome. CRA = concrete-representational-abstract. HFA = high functioning autism. IBET = Integrated Behavioral Experiential Teaching. NLD = nonverbal learning disability.

operations, self-regulation may be an appropriate strategy. Direct instruction may aid the student who is at a loss when deciding which strategy to pursue when confronted with an ambiguous mathematical situation. Direct instruction offers explicit strategies that the student can memorize and apply to different scenarios. Goal structure benefits students who struggle to know when they are finished, what successful completion means, and how to monitor their progress.

If a student has difficulty with the basic idea of a number and counting, CRA would help to establish that concept. IBET can be utilized at the earliest stages of learning, when the students are forming or reforming number concepts. Students with strong negative associations toward mathematics may benefit from using IBET to create positive associations with the discipline, integrating their own experiences into instruction, relating learning to meaningful life experiences, and forming a bridge between content to be learned and students' existing knowledge base (Zager, 2006).

The literature centering on mathematics interventions for students with HFA/AS has been sparse to date, although there is a growing discussion of the similarity of NLD to HFA/AS (e.g., Joseph et al., 2002; Williams et al., 2008). The strategies presented in this article have taken into consideration learning differences and similarities of students with NLD and HFA to provide useful insight into instructional design, and both populations may benefit.

## REFERENCES

American Psychiatric Association. (2000). *Diagnostic and statistical manual of mental disorders: DSM-IV-TR* (Text rev.; 4th ed.). Washington, DC: American Psychiatric Publishing.

Bos, C. S., & Vaughn, S. (2002). *Strategies for teaching students with learning and behavior problems.* Boston, MA: Allyn & Bacon.

Dunlap, L. K., & Dunlap, G. (1989). A self-monitoring package for teaching subtraction with regrouping to students with learning disabilities. *Journal of Applied Behavior Analysis, 22,* 309–314.

Fuchs, L. S., Bahr, C. M., & Rieth, H. J. (1989). Effects of goal structures and performance contingencies on the math performance of adolescents with learning disabilities. *Journal of Learning Disabilities, 22,* 554–560.

Goldstein, G., Beers, S. R., Siegel, D. J., & Minshew, N. J. (2001). A comparison of WAIS-R profiles in adults with high-functioning autism or differing subtypes of learning disability. *Applied Neuropsychology, 8*(3), 148–154.

Joseph, R. M., Tager-Flusberg, H., & Lord, C. (2002). Cognitive profiles and social-communicative functioning in children with autism spectrum disorder. *Journal of Child Psychology and Psychiatry, 43*(6), 807–821.

Klin, A., Volkmar, F. R., Sparrow, S. S., Cicchetti, D. V., & Rourke, B. P. (1995). Validity and neuropsychological characterization of Asperger syndrome: Convergence with nonverbal learning disabilities syndrome. *Journal of Child Psychology and Psychiatry, 36*(7), 1127–1140.

Macintosh, K. E., & Dissanayake, C. (2004). The similarities and differences between autistic disorder and Asperger's disorder: A review of the empirical evidence. *Journal of Child Psychology and Psychiatry, 45*(3), 421–434.

Mayes, S. D., & Calhoun, S. L. (2003). Analysis of WISC-III, Stanford-Binet: IV, and academic achievement test scores in children with autism. *Journal of Autism and Developmental Disorders, 33*(3), 329–341.

Mayes, S. D., & Calhoun, S. L. (2005). Frequency of reading, math, and writing disabilities in children with clinical disorders. *Learning and Individual Differences, 16*(2), 145–157.

Miller, S. P., Butler, F. M., & Lee, K. (1998). Validated practices for teaching mathematics to students with learning disabilities: A review of the literature. *Focus on Exceptional Children, 31*(1), 1–24.

Miller, S. P., & Mercer, C. D. (1993a). Using a graduated word problem sequence to promote problem-solving skills. *Learning Disabilities Research & Practice, 8,* 169–174.

Miller, S. P., & Mercer, C. D. (1993b). Using data to learn about concrete–semi-concrete-abstract instruction for students with math disabilities. *Learning Disabilities Research & Practice, 8,* 89–96.

Minshew, N. J., Goldstein, G., Taylor, H. G., & Siegel, D. J. (1994). Academic achievement in high functioning autistic individuals. *Journal of Clinical and Experimental Neuropsychology, 16*(2), 261–270.

Novick, B. Z., & Arnold, M. M. (1988). *Fundamentals of clinical child neuropsychology*. Philadelphia, PA: Grune & Stratton.

Pelletier, P. M., Ahmad, S. A., & Rourke, B. P. (2001). Classification rules for basic phonological processing disabilities and nonverbal learning disabilities: Formulation and external validity. *Child Neuropsychology, 7*(2), 84–88.

Rourke, B. P. (1989). *Nonverbal learning disabilities: The syndrome and the model.* New York, NY: The Guilford Press.

Rourke, B. P., Fisk, J. L., & Strang, J. D. (1986). *Neuropsychological assessment of children: A treatment oriented approach.* New York, NY: The Guilford Press.

Rourke, B. P., & Strang, J. D. (1978). Neuropsychological significance of variations in patterns of academic performance: Motor, psychomotor, and tactile-perceptual abilities. *Journal of Pediatric Psychology, 3*(2), 62–66.

Rourke, B. P., & Tsatsanis, K. D. (2000). Nonverbal learning disabilities and Asperger syndrome. In A. Klin, F. R. Volkmar, & S. S. Sparrow (Eds.), *Asperger syndrome* (pp. 231–253). New York, NY: The Guilford Press.

Spreen, O., Risser, A. T., & Edgell, D. (1995). *Developmental neuropsychology.* New York, NY: Oxford University Press.

Szatmari, P., Tuff, L., Finlayson, A., & Bartolucci, G. (1990). Asperger's syndrome and autism: Neurocognitive aspects. *Journal of the American Academy of Child & Adolescent Psychiatry, 29*(1), 130–136.

Van Houten, R., & Rolider, A. (1990). The use of color mediation techniques to teach number identification and single digit multiplication problems to children with learning problems. *Education and Treatment of Children, 13,* 216–224.

Williams, D. L., Goldstein, G., Kojkowski, N., & Minshew, N. J. (2008). Do individuals with high functioning autism have the IQ profile associated with nonverbal learning disability? *Research in Autism Spectrum Disorders, 2*(2), 353–361.

Wilson, C. L., & Sindelar, P. T. (1991). Direct instruction in math word problems: Students with learning disabilities. *Exceptional Children, 57,* 512–519.

Witzel, B. (2005). Using CRA to teach algebra to students with math difficulties in inclusive settings. *Learning Disabilities: A Contemporary Journal, 3*(2), 49–60.

Zager, D. (2006, December). *Integrated behavioral experiential teaching.* Paper presented at the The Rebecca School, New York, NY.

Zager, D. (2007, November). *Evidence-based practices in autism.* Paper presented at the annual meeting of the Arkansas Council for Exceptional Children, Hot Springs, AK.

Zager, D., & Gattasse, M. (2004, April). *Integrated behavioral experiential teaching (IBET) for students with autism.* Paper presented at the annual meeting of the International Council for Exceptional Children, Baltimore, MD.

Originally published in *TEACHING Exceptional Children,* Vol. 42, No. 6, pp. 40–46.

# 7

# Using Visual Script Interventions to Address Communication Skills

*Jennifer B. Ganz*

*Visual scripts and related educational strategies such as video modeling and social script narratives provide visual or auditory cues to promote communication and social skills in children with disabilities. Visual scripts are particularly useful for teachers who work with children with learning disabilities, autism spectrum disorders, and cognitive impairments—both students with average language skills and those with limited verbal skills. What are the benefits of visual scripts? Which student populations benefit most from their use? How does a teacher go about implementing a visual script?*

## WHAT ARE VISUAL SCRIPT INTERVENTIONS?

Visual scripts are written and pictorial examples of phrases or sentences children with disabilities can use to cue themselves regarding appropriate topics of conversation or other verbal interactions. Visual script interventions have been shown to be effective with children with autism, including those with minimal language (e.g., single spoken words, Krantz & McClannahan, 1998) and those with extensive verbal skills but poor social skills (Krantz & McClannahan, 1993); they are often used with children with autism spectrum disorders (Ganz, Cook, & Earles-Vollrath, 2006). Visual scripts are also appropriate for use with children with a variety of communication or social deficits. Scripts can be simple reminders of the words needed to get assistance (e.g., "help," accompanied by a picture), or provide suggestions for phrases to initiate conversations (e.g., "what's up?" or "what did you do last night?"). Scripts specific to units of study can help children with speech-language deficits or mild mental retardation expand their vocabulary. Students with learning disabilities or attention deficit/hyperactivity disorder (ADHD) may find visual scripts helpful in social situations to provide them with age- and socially-appropriate phrases (e.g., phrases useful for asking to join a play activity). Additionally, for children with emotional or behavioral disorders, scripts can promote the use of socially appropriate phrases to replace inappropriate language (e.g., cursing, slang). Students with disabilities who also have limited English proficiency may benefit from visual scripts that include current idioms or slang used by their peers.

## WHAT DOES THE LITERATURE SAY?

Much of the research supporting the use of scripts demonstrates their use with children with autism spectrum disorders (Charlop-Christy & Kelso, 2003; Krantz & McClannahan, 1993; Krantz & McClannahan, 1998; Sarokoff, Taylor, & Poulson, 2001; Stevenson, Krantz, & McClannahan, 2000) or with such children and their typically developing peers (Goldstein & Cisar, 1992); however, most of this research was conducted with small pools of participants. Research on script interventions (see Table 1) has demonstrated their efficacy with children with a range of abilities, from those with limited verbal abilities (i.e., single-word utterances and minimal reading skills; Krantz & McClannahan, 1998) to those who could speak in complete sentences but had limited use of social skills such as initiating conversations (Krantz & McClannahan, 1993). Scripts have been used to increase initiations toward adults (Charlop-Christy & Kelso; Krantz & McClannahan, 1998); initiations toward peers (Goldstein & Cisar; Krantz & McClannahan, 1993; Sarokoff et al.); requests for attention (Krantz & McClannahan, 1998); unprompted and unscripted statements (Krantz & McClannahan, 1993; Sarokoff et al.); question asking (Krantz & McClannahan, 1993); conversational statements about present items (Sarakoff et al.)  and about past or abstract events (Charlop-Christy & Kelso); responding to questions (Charlop-Christy & Kelso; Krantz & McClannahan, 1993); and use of sociodramatic play statements (Goldstein & Cisar). In each case, many or most of the new skills were maintained and generalized to novel settings, conversation partners, or materials.

## IMPLEMENTING VISUAL SCRIPTS

There are seven basic steps for implementing visual scripts (see Figure 1); the process itself is flexible and adaptable to the ability level and needs of the student (Ganz et al., 2006). Implementation of visual scripts involves choosing target activities and learner objectives, observing typically developing peers engaging in target activities and developing visual scripts, teaching the student

**Table 1. Research on Script Interventions**

| Study | Participants | Summary |
|---|---|---|
| Charlop-Christy & Kelso (2003) | 3 participants 8–11 years old | Participants were taught to use question-and-answer scripts consisting of abstract, non-present topics of conversation with an adult; children quickly learned correct scripted responses; many skills were maintained and generalized to new topics of conversation, trainers, and settings |
| Goldstein & Cisar (1992) | 9 participants (3 with characteristics of autism) 3–5 years old | Children were taught sociodramatic play scripts in triads with peers (2 typically developing children with 1 child with a disability); trainers gave verbal prompts/cues; participants learned scripts quickly; social behaviors (e.g., scripted phrases, words, and nonverbal behaviors, and nonscripted behaviors) increased; available online: http://www.pubmedcentral.nih.gov/ picrender.fcgi?artid = 1279709&blobtype = pdf |
| Krantz & McClannahan (1993) | 4 participants 9–12 years old | Participants were taught to use 10-line scripts to initiate social conversations with peers; scripts were faded over five steps; participants' use of scripted phrases increased and unscripted phrases and responses increased after scripts were faded; available online: http://www.pubmedcentral.nih.gov/picrender.fcgi? artid = 1297725&blobtype = pdf |
| Krantz & McClannahan (1998) | 3 participants 4–5 years old | Written cues were inserted in visual schedules and early-reader participants who used few verbal initiations were prompted to approach an adult and say the script; participants increased their use of scripted phrases, elaborations on scripted phrases, and novel initiations; skills generalized to novel activities; available online: http://www.pubmedcentral.nih.gov/picrender.fcgi? artid = 1284111&blobtype = pdf |
| Sarokoff, Taylor, & Poulson (2001) | 2 participants 8–9 years old | Participants who could read were taught embedded text that corresponded with snack and play items; scripts were faded after they were mastered; participants increased use of scripted statements and maintained their use after scripts were faded; unscripted statements increased; all statements generalized to new items and peers; available online: http://www. pubmedcentral.nih.gov/picrender.fcgi?artid = 1284302&blobtype = pdf |
| Stevenson, Krantz, & McClannahan, (2000) | 4 participants 10–15 years old | Participants could use expressive language to make requests, use greetings, and respond to demands or questions but infrequently used spontaneous conversational speech; they were taught to engage in conversations regarding present items; participants mastered scripts rapidly, increased the number of unscripted statements, and maintained their use after prompts and scripts were faded |

**Figure 1. Steps for Implementing Visual Scripts**

**Step 1:** Choose a target activity

**Step 2:** Observe typically developing children

**Step 3:** Choose a learning objective

**Step 4:** Write the script

**Step 5:** Teach the script

**Step 6:** Implement the script during the target activity

**Step 7:** Fade the script

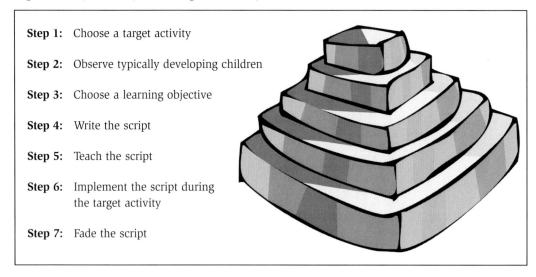

to recite the script, and implementing then fading the use of the script. Scripts are most successful when they incorporate student interests and familiar activities and settings and they are easily adapted for a variety of student ability levels and within numerous environments.

## Step 1: Choose a Target Activity

Script interventions are most successful if the target activity is something the student enjoys and is motivated to engage in. What are the student's interests? Are there any solitary activities that the student has already mastered that can be converted into social activities? (For example, Polo could already take his lunch out of his lunch box, sit in his seat, unwrap each item, eat his lunch, and throw away his trash independently; however, he never spoke to his classmates despite sitting next to them for 2 months.) What activities do typically developing children engage in that the target student does not, because he or she lacks the social or communication skills? Activities that are popular with the student's peers are good choices for intervention, particularly if an overarching goal is to increase opportunities to integrate the child into settings with typically developing peers.

## Step 2: Observe Typically Developing Children Engaging in the Activity

Note comments they make, how they initiate conversations, questions they ask, and topics of conversation. It may help to observe during at least three occasions, each time writing verbatim what the child's peers say. This information will assist in determining necessary skills for the child to participate in

**Table 2.  Visual Script Scenarios and Learning Objectives**

| Scenarios | Learning Objectives/Skills |
|---|---|
| Playing board games | • Social greetings<br>• Asking for a turn<br>• Comments necessary to play the game |
| Constructive play | • Social greetings<br>• Offering a toy<br>• Asking for help<br>• Complimenting playmates<br>• Comments on current activities |
| Sociodramatic play | • Social greetings<br>• Offering a toy<br>• Complimenting playmates<br>• Pretend-play scripts |
| Eating a meal or snack | • Offering to share<br>• Comments regarding past events<br>• Comments regarding abstract topics<br>• Using humor<br>• Responding to peers' comments/questions |
| Vocational tasks | • Asking for help<br>• Asking for materials<br>• Comments on current activities |
| Playing a sport | • Comments appropriate for the sport<br>• Cheering for teammates<br>• Responding to peers' comments/questions |

the target activity and will help determine what phrases should be included in the script.

## Step 3: Choose a Learning Objective

Before writing the script, determine a specific, measurable learning objective—or more than one, depending on the ability level of the student (Ganz et al., 2006). Learning objectives may be chosen from the child's individualized education program (IEP) or may be activity-specific. Table 2 provides a list of possible scenarios and corresponding learning objectives.

## Step 4: Write the Script

The length and complexity of the script depends on the ability level of the student (Ganz et al., 2006). Reflecting on information gathered during the observation of typically developing peers engaging in the chosen activity, write a list of sentences or phrases that the student will learn to use during the social activity.

## Step 5: Teach the Script

The student will need to be able to repeat the visual script sentences or phrases fluently (Ganz et al., 2006). Depending on the reading abilities of the student, the entire script may be taught in one sitting or over several days. At this point, the script may need to be adjusted. For example, Jason was having difficulty remembering 10 phrases and was not able to read them fluently after six sessions of instruction, so his teacher decreased the script to six phrases and added small line drawings to help him remember each phrase.

## Step 6: Implement the Script

During the target activity, present the script (Ganz et al., 2006; Krantz & McClannhan, 1993). Scripts may be written on note cards or on paper, and include a means for the student to keep track of phrases used, such as check-off boxes in front of each phrase (Krantz & McClannahan, 1993), crossing phrases off a list, or using flip cards of phrases on a key ring.

## Step 7: Fade the Script

The script can be kept in place if the student relies heavily on visual cues. If possible, however, the script should be faded over time (Ganz et al., 2006). This can be done over several steps. Krantz and McClannahan (1993) recommend removing the script a piece at a time, first removing ending punctuation, then removing portions of the phrases, starting at the end, eventually leaving only bullets or check boxes. Script fading may take place rapidly or over several weeks, depending on the student's memory skills (Ganz et al.).

Following the implementation of scripts in a number of social situations, the scripts may be faded altogether. However, teachers should periodically collect observational data on the skills acquired as a result of scripts and, if necessary, reintroduce the scripts if the skills were not maintained. Some students begin to use novel phrases as the scripts are faded, whereas others may require implementation of scripts spanning several months.

## Variations

**Length of the Phrases.** Phrases should be kept to one to two words for children who can speak only in short phrases, but should be lengthier for students with stronger verbal and reading skills. Similarly, early readers and those with minimal verbal skills should be given only a few phrases—possibly only 1 word or phrase—per script; students with stronger reading and verbal skills can use scripts with 10 or more phrases.

**Script Format.** The script can be audiotaped, written, video, or verbally cued, depending on the student's learning style. Scripts may include pictures, photographs or line drawings, to assist nonreaders or early readers in remembering the script phrases, or may include only text for fluent readers. In addition to the variety of ways to identify which phrases have been used earlier, a teacher or aide can hold up phrase cards for students who are unable to use scripts independently. Teachers can modify any of these areas if the student is having difficulty reading or remembering the script, can shorten the script, use larger text, or add pictures.

## SCRIPT SCENARIOS

### Isa

Isa was a kindergartener with developmental delays and speech impairment attending a general education kindergarten classroom for about half of the day, including lunch, physical education, music, center time, and story time. The rest of the day she was in a self-contained special education classroom where she received intensive one-on-one and small-group instruction. She could speak in one to two-word phrases, answer simple questions, and follow one-step directions; however, she rarely initiated conversations with peers in her kindergarten class, and her vocabulary was significantly limited compared to her peers. During center time, Isa usually played with the blocks. She had previously been taught to make towers and roads to drive cars on, which she did independently. Though other children often played in the same center, Isa did not interact with them. Isa's teacher, Mrs. Malone, chose playing with blocks as the target activity (Step 1). Before writing Isa's script, Mrs. Malone watched a few groups of kindergarteners play in the block center over several days and wrote down the phrases they used (e.g., "Here, you can have the long block," "Look at this!"; Step 2). Isa's IEP objectives included sharing toys and expressively identifying shapes, so Mrs. Malone chose those as Isa's main learning objectives (Step 3): Isa would be expected to hand a block to a peer, Sarah, and say, "circle block," "rectangle block," or "square block." (Mrs. Malone chose Sarah to be Isa's play partner because she had shown an interest in Isa and often asked to be her helper during Isa's time in the kindergarten classroom.) Next, Mrs. Malone wrote a script for Isa (Step 4; see Figure 2). Prior to implementing the script, Mrs. Malone played in the block center with Sarah for several days, showing her the script, modeling each line, and having Isa repeat each phrase and hand her the identified block (Step 5). Finally, Mrs. Malone implemented the script with Isa and Sarah (Step 6). The teacher began by taking Isa's hand and helping her point to each line on the script, then prompting by holding Isa's arm, and eventually removing any physical or gestured prompts. After Isa was

**Figure 2. Isa's Script**

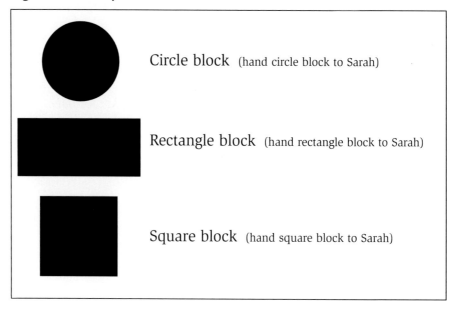

using the script independently, Mrs. Malone faded its use (Step 7); Isa began spontaneously offering blocks to Sarah without looking toward the script.

## Thomas

Thomas was an eighth-grader with a learning disability and ADHD; he could speak in complete sentences, with grammar and vocabulary at a level comparable to his peers, but had difficulty determining topics of conversation and often sat alone at lunch and other free periods, talking to no one. He attended general education classes and only received special education for content mastery (e.g., as needed for content area instruction and independent work) and for social skills instruction twice a week. Thomas wanted to make friends and have someone to talk to at lunch, so he and his teacher, Mr. Laine, chose eating lunch as a target activity (Step 1). Mr. Laine observed other eighth-grade boys (Step 2) and he and Thomas decided to work on making context-appropriate comments (Step 3), and together wrote a script (Step 4; see Figure 3). Immediately before each lunch period, Thomas would fill in most of the blanks with appropriate words or phrases. His script included more abstract expectations than Isa's because of his verbal and cognitive strengths. Because Thomas was a fluent reader, he quickly mastered reading his script and checking off each box as he used a phrase (Step 5). Mr. Laine sat far enough away at the lunch table to be discreet, but close enough to hear Thomas and his peers during lunch (Step 6). Finally, Mr. Laine used a script fading procedure to remove portions of each phrase on the script, starting at the end of each sentence, until Thomas was using novel phrases (Step 7).

**Figure 3. Thomas's Script**

Talk about what your friends are talking about.

❏   Hi, guys.

❏   What did you bring for lunch today, ____ (name of friend)?

❏   I brought ____ (something in your lunch sack).

❏   I like ____ (something to eat).

❏   Do you like ___ (something to eat)?

❏   *(make a comment about what a friend is talking about)*

Written scripts are a promising practice in improving social and communication skills in children with deficits in those areas. They can be modified for almost any age or ability level, offering a means of support to the wide variety of students who receive special education.

# REFERENCES

Charlop-Christy, M. H., & Kelso, S. E., (2003). Teaching children with autism conversational speech using a cue card/written script program. *Education and Treatment of Children, 26,* 108–127.

Ganz, J. B., Cook, K. E., & Earles-Vollrath, T. L. (2006). *How to write and implement social script interventions* (Autism Spectrum Disorder Series). Austin, TX: Pro-Ed.

Goldstein, H., & Cisar, C. L. (1992). Promoting interaction during sociodramatic play: Teaching scripts to typical preschoolers and classmates with disabilities. *Journal of Applied Behavior Analysis, 25,* 265–280.

Krantz, P. J., & McClannahan, L. E. (1993). Teaching children with autism to initiate to peers: Effects of a script-fading procedure. *Journal of Applied Behavior Analysis, 26,* 121–132.

Krantz, P. J., & McClannahan, L. E. (1998). Social interaction skills for children with autism: A script-fading procedure for beginning readers. *Journal of Applied Behavior Analysis, 31,* 191–202.

Sarokoff, R. A., Taylor, B. A., & Poulson, C. L. (2001). Teaching children with autism to engage in conversational exchanges: Script fading with embedded textual stimuli. *Journal of Applied Behavior Analysis, 34,* 81–84

Stevenson, C. L., Krantz, P. J., & McClannahan, L. E. (2000). Social interaction skills for children with autism: A script-fading procedure for nonreaders. *Behavioral Interventions, 15,* 1–20.

Originally published in *TEACHING Exceptional Children,* Vol. 40, No. 2, pp. 54–58.

# 8

# Video Modeling Strategies to Enhance Appropriate Behaviors in Children With Autism Spectrum Disorders

*Devender R. Banda, Rose Marie Matuszny, and Sultan Turkan*

*Since September, Suzan, a special educator, had been working on communication and socialization skills with John, one of her students who was diagnosed with autism. Suzan recognized that John had made little progress over the first 3 months of school participating in interventions such as peer modeling and verbal explanations of effective communication and socialization skills. She decided to seek suggestions from her colleagues about possible other evidence-based interventions that might be more effective for students with autism. Luckily, Suzan found one colleague who had recently attended a workshop on video modeling. Her colleague shared with her that the intervention was evidence-based and effective for teaching various skills to students with autism. Suzan was grateful for the information and was especially excited about its potential because John particularly enjoys watching television and videos.*

Video modeling (VM) is one of the strategies that may help teachers like Suzan increase appropriate behaviors among children with autism spectrum disorders (ASD). Children with ASD exhibit deficits in the areas of communication, socialization, behavior, and other life skills (Scott, Clark, & Brady, 2000). Teachers need strategies that are evidence-based to improve these skills in children with autism. The use of evidence-based strategies is important because it is required by the No Child Left Behind Act of 2001 (NCLB) and reduces unnecessary costs and resources related to interventions that have not been supported by research (Ellis & Fouts, 1997; Scott et al.; Simpson, 2005). Furthermore, evidence-based practices are important because they have been thoroughly researched by numerous investigators in different settings and with different individuals. Research indicates that the VM strategy has been effective for improving various skill deficits in the areas of communication, socialization, academics, and daily living (Ayres & Langone, 2005). The VM intervention involves showing a videotape or DVD of a person who demonstrates the exact version of a target behavior. The child who watches the video or DVD is then expected to imitate the demonstrated behavior (LeBlanc et al., 2003). The VM intervention may be one of the preferred strategies for teachers to use because children with ASD learn tasks through visual modes (see Buggey, 2005; Pierce & Schreibman, 1994; Quill, 1997), and watching television may be a highly reinforcing activity (Charlop-Christy & Daneshvar, 2003). Additionally, there are several other benefits associated with the use of VM interventions.

The VM strategy is nonaversive (Sturmey, 2003), and many parents and teachers view it as an acceptable intervention (see Buggey, Toombs, Gardener, & Cervetti 1999; Charlop & Milstein, 1989; Nikopoulos & Keenan, 2003). VM interventions are convenient for parents and teachers because recorded videotapes/DVDs can be reused. Furthermore, teachers may have better control over the type of behaviors that are presented to children; unwanted behaviors may be edited. Likewise, research indicates that video models are advantageous over in vivo models, because video models are more likely than "in vivo" models to enhance maintenance and promote generalization of learned skills (e.g., communication, daily living, and socialization; see Charlop-Christy, Le, & Freeman, 2000). In addition, VM interventions are economical for teachers when instructing community living skills such as purchasing grocery items (Alcantara, 1994); these skills can be modeled and recorded on videotape or DVD and shown to children initially to provide a less invasive intervention before they practice the skills in real life settings.

Research on VM interventions with children with ASD indicates that several behaviors can be targeted. The behaviors include socialization (e.g., greeting others, standing in a line in the cafeteria, sharing toys, turn-taking); communication (e.g., initiating conversation, requesting, asking questions, answering questions, and commenting); and functional living skills (e.g., riding a bus, going to a grocery store, shaving). The VM intervention can be considered an evidence-based teaching strategy because researchers in several studies consistently found it to be effective for children with ASD. See Figure 1 to review additional information regarding what the literature says about VM interventions with children with ASD.

There is sufficient evidence to indicate that VM interventions are useful for children with ASD. However, it is important that teachers be provided explicit and simple procedures in order to efficiently and effectively implement these interventions in schools and/or clinical settings. Following, we present several important steps that teachers can use when employing VM interventions to enhance the social and communication skills of children with

**Figure 1. What Does the Literature Say About VM Interventions With Children With Autism?**

Research indicates that VM has been very effective in increasing the following skills in persons with ASD:

*Daily Living Skills*

- Setting a table, preparing orange juice, preparing a letter to be mailed (Shipley-Benamou, Lutzker, & Taubman, 2002).
- Meal preparation (Rehfeldt, Dahman, Young, Cherry, & Davis, 2003).
- Shaving, making a bed, hanging pants/shirts (Lasater & Brady, 1995).
- Purchasing (Alcantara, 1994; Haring, Kennedy, Adams, & Pitts-Conway, 1987).
- Brushing teeth (Charlop-Christy, & Freeman, 2000).
- Microwave oven use (Sigafoos, O'Reilly, Cannella, Upadhyaya, & Edirisinha, 2005).

*Communication Skills*

- Spontaneous requesting (Wert & Neisworth, 2003)
- Recognizing emotions in speech and facial expressions (Corbett, 2003)
- Compliment-giving initiations and responses (Apple, Billingsley, & Schwartz, 2005)
- Language production (Buggey, 2005; Charlop-Christy et al., 2000)
- Verbal responses to questions (Buggey et al., 1999)
- Conversational speech  (Charlop & Milstein, 1989; Charlop-Christy et al., 2000; Nikopoulos & Keenan, 2003, 2004; Ogeltree & Fischer, 1995; Sherer, Pierce,  Parades, Kisacky, & Ingersoll, 2001).

*Social Skills*

- Play behaviors including reciprocal play (Nikopoulos & Keenan, 2004); motor and verbal play sequences (D'Ateno, Mangiapanello, & Taylor, 2003); independent play (Charlop-Christy et al., 2000); play-related comments (Taylor, Levin, & Jasper, 1999); and socio-dramatic play (Dauphin, Kinney, & Stromer, 2004; Nikopoulos & Keenan, 2003)
- Complying, greeting, and sharing (Simpson, Langone, & Ayres, 2004)
- Spontaneous greeting (Charlop-Christy et al., 2000)
- Social initiations  (Nikopoulos & Keenan, 2004; Buggey, 2005)

*Academics*

- Generative spelling (Kinney, Vedora, & Stromer, 2003).

*Inappropriate Behaviors*

- Aggressive pushing and tantrums (Buggey, 2005)

**Figure 2. Steps for Conducting VM Interventions**

1. Identify and Select Target Behaviors
2. Obtain Necessary Permissions
3. Interview Parents and Observe the Child
4. Select and Train Models
5. Prepare Equipment and Setting
6. Record Target Behaviors (Model's)
7. Edit the Video
8. Collect Baseline Data
9. Show the Video Clip of Desired Behaviors
10. Collect Intervention Data and Graph Data
11. Promote Maintenance and Generalization

ASD. We selected these skills because researchers have consistently found that VM strategies enhance and facilitate the generalization of social and communication behaviors of children with ASD (e.g., Ayres & Langone, 2005; Buggey et al., 1999).

## STEPS FOR CONDUCTING VM INTERVENTIONS

VM interventions need to be conducted systematically to improve target behaviors. In the following sections, we present several steps. (See Figure 2.) Each step is based on available research and good teaching and evaluation practices, and each is described in detail and paired with relevant examples. We have also added an example of a data collection sheet and graph that can be used for monitoring and evaluating student progress.

### Step 1: Identify and Select Target Behaviors

It is important to precisely identify and define target behaviors that are observable and measurable. For example, identifying communication skills as the target behavior is not precise enough. Initiating communicative behaviors such as waving hands or saying "hello" to an adult or peer are more precise definitions of a target behavior because they can be observed and measured. We suggest that teachers select communication or social skills for improvement because of overwhelming research support. However, teachers should use caution when selecting problem behaviors for decrease because very few studies have been conducted using VM techniques to decrease problem behaviors in children with ASD (Buggey, 2005; Simpson et al., 2004).

## Step 2: Obtain Necessary Permissions

We recommend that the VM strategy be planned and implemented only after obtaining necessary permissions from the school. In addition, teachers should obtain a signed informed consent from parents to ensure the protection of participants' rights and confidentiality. Also, storage of videotapes and access to videos must be kept confidential (Meharg & Woltersdorf, 1990). It is recommended that teachers or related professionals destroy or erase videotapes after the intervention is complete and the student has mastered the target skill, unless there is mutual consensus between parents and teachers to retain them for future use.

## Step 3: Interview Parents and Observe the Child

Not all children with ASD show interest in watching TV. Therefore, it is crucial to conduct a formal or informal assessment of the student's interest in watching TV or other video recorded material. Simple interview questions can be posed to parents about the child's interests and/or recreational activities (e.g., Does the child like to watch TV? Does the child watch her/his birthday videos? Does the child like to watch cartoons or kids channels?). Another option would entail the teacher observing the child in the classroom or in the library as the child watches different videos or DVDs and assessing the student's attention to and preferences for the videos. We recommend direct observation in addition to parental interview to get an accurate assessment of the child's preferences/ interests.

## Step 4: Select and Train Models

An important step in the VM intervention procedure is careful selection of video models who can clearly demonstrate the target behavior. Research shows that models may vary, including the student herself/himself (e.g., Lasater & Brady, 1995; Wert & Neisworth, 2003); peers (e.g., Buggey, 2005; Corbett, 2003; Haring et al., 1987); familiar adults (e.g., Kinney et al., 2003; LeBlanc et al., 2003); and cartoons (Ogeltree & Fischer, 1995). Particularly, when children are selected as models, the teacher must make sure that they clearly and consistently display appropriate target behaviors in natural environments. For example, if you have a child who does not get along with other children, he/she may not be suitable for modeling social behaviors. Observe the model and decide whether the model precisely imitates the target behaviors. Also, it is highly recommended and required that teachers train models; the training should include explicit modeling of target behaviors, practice, and evaluation of the target behavior. Teachers should prepare a script and have the model practice several times until the child feels comfortable. If necessary, rehearse with the model.

## Step 5: Prepare Equipment and Setting

A digital camcorder or VHS-C camcorder may be used to record the model's behavior. The setting should be well lit so that the recorded images are clearly visible. Use a tripod to minimize excessive movement while recording. If the camera is powered by batteries, make sure to have backup batteries. Also, keep extra tapes or enough storage space available when using a digital camera. In addition, ensure that the setting does not include too many visually attractive materials (e.g., wall posters, bright colored objects), as they may divert the attention of children with ASD to irrelevant details.

## Step 6: Record Target Behaviors

Recording must be done when the model is trained and comfortable. Let the model know when you are ready to record and when you plan to pause or stop recording. Signal the model to display the target behavior. Make sure to record several sessions in order to capture clear target behaviors of the model to be presented to the child with ASD. Also, guard against unnecessary distractions when recording the target behavior. For example, when recording the video, other children or teachers may walk into the setting. It is also necessary to record only target behaviors; recording other behaviors, although appropriate, may confuse the child with ASD.

## Step 7: Edit the Video

There are several criteria to keep in mind while editing the recorded video. First, decide whether the behaviors of the model(s) look as natural as possible. Second, make sure that the pace of the video is normal—not too slow or too fast. Third, decide if the duration of the video is appropriate. The majority of researchers have used an average duration of 3 to 5 minutes for VM interventions, although, there have been reports of videos that were as short as 5 to 20 seconds (e.g., Corbett, 2003) and as long as 20 minutes (e.g., Lasater & Brady, 1995). Therefore, it is recommended that teachers use shorter duration videos ranging from 3 to 5 minutes. Fourth, if you have a child with limited communication abilities, you may want to include pauses/beeps in the video to provide clarity. This would also ensure that the student receives enough time to practice the behavior, or to allow the teacher to ask comprehension questions when necessary. Finally, the teacher should consider breaking the skill into small steps (i.e., task analysis), providing explicit demonstration of the skill, and prompting/reinforcing when working with a student with limited abilities (see Alcantara, 1994; Haring et al., 1987).

## Step 8: Collect Baseline Data

Collecting baseline data for the target behavior prior to showing the edited video is very crucial. It may help teachers to clearly identify the student's present level of functioning. Also, ongoing data collection helps teachers monitor students' progress and evaluate the effectiveness of the intervention strategy. You can either collect baseline data on the frequency or duration of behaviors. For example, a tally sheet could be created to indicate the number of times (i.e., frequency) the child requests, initiates, or greets an adult (i.e., communication behaviors). Duration data may be collected on how long the student with ASD plays with a peer or adult while sharing toys or participating in a pretend play (i.e., social skills). We recommend that baseline data be collected for a minimum of 3 to 4 sessions/days to obtain baseline stability. Figures 3 and 4, respectively, provide examples of a baseline data sheet and graph. After collecting baseline, begin the VM intervention by showing the edited video clip(s) to the child with ASD.

## Step 9: Show the Video Clip of Desired Behaviors

Select a specific place and time to show the video to the child with ASD. Make sure that any possible interruptions are eliminated around the video showing arena. Also, plan well in advance where to pause/stop the video, when to ask comprehension questions, or where to reinforce student responses. Even though there is no research available on the size of the screen, we recommend that, for demonstration purposes, teachers use a 21 inch or larger screen.

Following the video demonstration, the teacher may ask the child with ASD to perform the desired behaviors observed on the video. Make certain to have the child imitate the target behavior in a setting that is similar to that shown in the video. If the student exhibits or attempts to exhibit the target behavior, reward the behavior (e.g., edibles, tokens, praise, hug, and "high-five"). If the student does not demonstrate the target behavior, provide prompting (physical or verbal). If required, replay the video clip(s) to provide more opportunities for the child with ASD to view and practice the target behavior.

## Step 10: Collect Intervention Data and Graph Data

Collect data during the intervention period when the child demonstrates the target behavior observed on the video. Plot the data using a simple line graph. We provided a hypothetical sample data sheet for frequency of communication behaviors and a corresponding graph for further clarification. See Figure 3 for sample data collection for John and Figure 4 to view a simple graph indicating sample communication behaviors in a child with ASD before and after intervention.

## Step 11: Promote Maintenance and Generalization

If the VM intervention strategy is working, continue the intervention and reinforce the target behaviors. It is also critical for teachers to train children with ASD to generalize learned skills to other people, settings, or behaviors. For example, if the child initiates communication with a peer consistently over a

**Figure 3. An Example of Frequency Data Collection Sheet for John's Greeting Behavior**

Data Collection Sheet

Name of Student: *John*

Target Behavior: *Greeting behavior in a hallway including "hello," "hi"*

| Date | Time | Frequency of "hello"/"Hi" | Total |
|------|------|---------------------------|-------|
| **Baseline** | | | |
| 05-02-06 | 8:30 – 9 am | I | 1 |
| 05-03-06 | 8:30 – 9 am | I | 1 |
| 05-04-06 | 8:30 – 9 am | | |
| **Video Modeling by Peer** | | | |
| 05-06-06 | 8:30 – 9 am | JHT | 4 |
| 05-07-06 | 8:30 – 9 am | JHT I | 6 |
| 05-08-06 | 8:30 – 9 am | JHT II | 7 |
| 05-09-06 | 8:30 – 9 am | JHT | 5 |
| 05-10-06 | 8:30 – 9 am | JHT III | 8 |

period of time (2–3 weeks) after watching the video, it would be appropriate to include more peers in the process and see whether or not the student initiates conversations with the other peers. Also, the teacher can take the student to a different setting (e.g., from the classroom to the cafeteria) and determine if the child communicates with other students in different settings. Prompts may be necessary if the student does not initiate conversation in the new setting or with new peers. If the student is successful, reinforce the behaviors so that the student is more likely to initiate communication or social behaviors with others.

## FINAL THOUGHTS

The VM intervention is an evidence-based teaching strategy that may help children with ASD develop or improve several communication and socialization skills when implemented systematically as described here. VM interventions may be more economical for teachers because they could use the strategy not only with the target student but also with other students who display similar skill deficits. It is important that educators understand that it will take some time to become efficient in implementing this strategy, because of the technologies involved. By following the steps provided here, teachers are

**Figure 4. A Sample Graph Showing Greeting Behaviors During Baseline and Video Model Intervention**

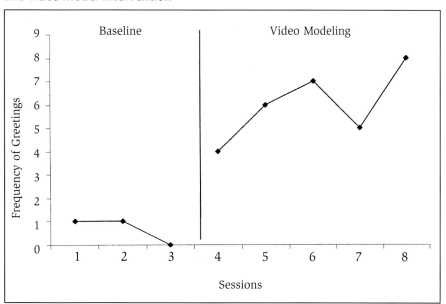

more likely to see their students with ASD experience successful intervention results while maintaining teaching efficiency and enhanced instructional time.

## REFERENCES

Alcantara, P. R. (1994). Effects of videotape instructional package on purchasing skills of children with autism. *Exceptional Children, 61*, 40–55.

Apple, A. L., Billingsley, F., & Schwartz, I. S. (2005). Effects of video modeling alone and with self-management on compliment-giving behaviors of children with high-functioning ASD. *Journal of Positive Behavior Interventions, 7*, 33–46.

Ayres, K. M., & Langone, J. (2005). Intervention and instruction with video for students with autism: A review of literature. *Education and Training in Developmental Disabilities, 40*, 183–196.

Buggey, T. (2005). Video self-modeling applications with students with autism spectrum disorder in a small private school setting. *Focus on Autism and Other Developmental Disabilities, 20*, 52–63.

Buggey, T., Toombs, K., Gardener, P., & Cervetti, M. (1999). Training responding behaviors in students with autism: Using videotaped self-modeling. *Journal of Positive Behavior Interventions, 1*, 205–214.

Charlop, M. H., & Milstein, J. P. (1989). Teaching autistic children conversational speech using video modeling. *Journal of Applied Behavior Analysis, 22*, 275–285.

Charlop-Christy, M. H., & Daneshvar, S. (2003). Using video modeling to teach perspective taking to children with autism. *Journal of Positive Behavior Interventions, 5*, 12–21.

Charlop-Christy, M. H., Le, L., & Freeman, K. A. (2000). A comparison of video modeling with in vivo modeling for teaching children with autism. *Journal of Autism & Developmental Disorders, 30,* 537–552.

Corbett, B. A. (2003). Video modeling: A window into the world of autism. *The Behavior Analyst Today, 4,* 88–96.

D'Ateno, P., Mangiapanello, K., & Taylor, B. A. (2003). Using video modeling to teach complex play sequences to a preschooler with autism. *Journal of Positive Behavior Interventions, 5,* 5–11.

Dauphin, M., Kinney, E. M., & Stromer, R. (2004). Using video-enhanced activity schedules and matrix training to teach sociodramatic play to a child with autism. *Journal of Positive Behavior Interventions, 6,* 238–250.

Ellis, A. K., & Fouts, J. T. (1997). *Research on educational innovations* (2nd ed.). Larchmont, NY: Eye on Education.

Haring, T., Kennedy, C., Adams, M., & Pitts-Conway, V. (1987). Teaching generalization of purchasing skills across community settings to autistic youth using videotape modeling. *Journal of Applied Behavior Analysis, 20,* 89–96.

Kinney, E., Vedora, J., & Stromer, R. (2003). Computer-presented video models to teach generative spelling to a child with an autistic spectrum disorder. *Journal of Positive Behavior Interventions, 5,* 22–29.

Lasater, M. W., & Brady, M. P. (1995). Effects of video self-modeling and feedback on task fluency: A home-based intervention. *Education & Treatment of Children, 18,* 389–407.

LeBlanc, L. A., Coates, A. M., Daneshvar, S., Charlop-Christy, M. H., Morris, C., Lancaster B. M. (2003). Using video modeling and reinforcement to teach perspective-taking skills to children with autism. *Journal of Applied Behavior Analysis, 36,* 253–257.

Meharg, S. S., & Woltersdorf, M. A. (1990). Therapeutic use of videotape self-modeling. *Advances in Behavior Research & Therapy, 12,* 85–89.

Nikopoulos, C. K., & Keenan, M. (2003). Promoting social initiation in children with autism using video modeling. *Behavioral Interventions, 18,* 87–118.

Nikopoulos, C. K., & Keenan, M. (2004). Effects of video modeling on social initiations by children with autism. *Journal of Applied Behavior Analysis, 37,* 93–96.

Ogeltree, B. T., & Fischer, M. A. (1995). An innovative language treatment for a child with high functioning autism. *Focus on Autistic Behavior, 10,* 1–10.

Pierce, K., & Schreibman, L. (1994). Teaching daily living skills to children with autism in unsupervised settings through pictorial management. *Journal of Applied Behavior Analysis, 27,* 471–481.

Quill, K. A. (1997). Instructional considerations for young children with autism: The rationale for visually cued instruction. *Journal of Autism and Developmental Disabilities, 27,* 697–714.

Rehfeldt, R. A., Dahman, D., Young, A., Cherry, H., & Davis, P. (2003). Teaching a simple meal preparation skill to adults with moderate and severe mental retardation using video modeling. *Behavioral Intervention, 18,* 209–218.

Scott, J., Clark, C., & Brady, M. (2000). *Students with autism:  Characteristics and instruction programming.* San Diego, CA: Singular.

Sherer, M., Pierce, K. L., Parades, S., Kisacky, K. L., Ingersoll, B., & Schreibman, L., (2001). Enhancing conversation skills in children with autism via video technology: Which is better, "self" or "other" as a model? *Behavior Modification, 25,* 140–158.

Shipley-Benamou, R., Lutzker, J. R., & Taubman, M. (2002). Teaching daily living skills to children with autism through instructional video modeling. *Journal of Positive Behavior Interventions, 4,* 165–175.

Sigafoos, J., O'Reilly, M. J., Cannella, H., Upadhyaya, M., Edirisinha, C., Lancioni, G,. et al. (2005). Computer-presented video prompting for teaching microwave oven use to teach three adults with developmental disabilities. *Journal of Behavioral Education, 14,* 189–201.

Simpson, A., Langone, J., & Ayres, K. A. (2004). Embedded video and computer based instruction to improve social skills for students with autism. *Education and Training in Developmental Disabilities, 39,* 240–252.

Simpson, R. L. (2005). Evidence-based practices and students with autism spectrum disorders. *Focus on Autism and Other Developmental Disabilities, 20,* 140–149.

Sturmey, P. (2003). Video technology and persons with autism and other developmental disabilities: An emerging technology for PBS. *Journal of Positive Behavior Interventions, 5,* 3–4.

Taylor, B. A., Levin, L., & Jasper, S. (1999). Increasing play-related statements in children with autism toward their siblings: Effects of video modeling. *Journal of Developmental & Physical Disabilities, 11,* 253–264.

Wert, B. Y., & Neisworth, J. T. (2003). Effects of video self-modeling on spontaneous requesting in children with autism. *Journal of Positive Behavior Interventions, 5,* 30–34.

Originally published in *TEACHING Exceptional Children,* Vol. 39, No. 6, pp. 47–52.

# 9

# Activity Schedules: Helping Students With Autism Spectrum Disorders in General Education Classrooms Manage Transition Issues

*Devender R. Banda, Eric Grimmett, and Stephanie L. Hart*

*Kate, a first-grade general education teacher, has a new student with Asperger's syndrome in her classroom. John has a very difficult time moving from one activity to the next. Often he will simply refuse to transition to the next activity by sitting down on the floor and not moving. Other times he will scream and physically lash out at his peers and the teacher. Kate noticed that the problem behaviors usually occur during a change in his anticipated daily routines. These outbursts are very disruptive to the rest of the class, and some of the other students have begun to avoid John during classroom activities. John's parents report similar difficulties at home during transitions or changes in his schedule. Kate needs to find some research-based strategies to help John more readily accept changes in his schedule and daily activities.*

Refusing to transition from one activity to the next or between steps in a single activity can impact a student's academic progress, socialization, and independence. Problem behaviors during transitions can impact the effectiveness of teacher instruction and disrupt other students' activities. As a result, the child with the behavior problem may be excluded from peer social circles. Difficulty with transitions can significantly limit a student's ability to independently complete activities across environments throughout the school day (e.g., Forest, Horner, Lewis-Palmer, & Todd, 2004; Scheuermann & Webber, 2002; Schreibman, Whalen, & Stahmer, 2000).

Autism spectrum disorder (ASD) is characterized by a qualitative impairment in at least two of the three following areas: social interaction; communication; and restricted repetitive and stereotyped patterns of behavior, interests, and activities. In addition, individuals diagnosed with autism demonstrate delays or abnormal functioning with onset before age 3 in social interaction, language used for social communication, and/or symbolic or imaginative play (American Psychiatric Association, APA, 2000). Students diagnosed with ASD often struggle with transitions, which may lead to problem behaviors such as verbal and physical aggression, tantrums, noncompliance, and self-injury (Schreibman et al., 2000).

Transition problems can be especially evident when children with ASD are taught in general education settings. The Centers for Disease Control and Prevention (2007) report that the prevalence of ASD was approximately 1 in 150 children and reflects an increase in diagnoses and special education servicing of children eligible under "autism" designations over the past decade. Teachers can expect to face transition problems in the general education classroom with the inclusion of students with ASD, as a general education environment can be overwhelming to these children. The many different activities scheduled in a typical school day are problematic for a child whose resistance to change is an inherent component of his or her autism (e.g., APA, 2000; Schreibman et al., 2000). Further, many children with ASD have difficulties with communication and socialization, which may contribute to problem behaviors when facing both routine and unexpected schedule changes (Jamieson, 2004). To ease transitions, adults may opt to provide support for every change within a daily schedule. However, this may cause children with ASD to become overly dependent on adult caregivers to stay on task and on schedule throughout their daily activities (Heflin & Alaimo, 2007; Scheuermann & Webber, 2002). The challenge to teachers is to provide students with the needed support during transitions while decreasing dependence on adult instructions.

There are several strategies for reducing transition difficulties, such as choice making, incorporating preferred activities, using behavioral momentum or high-probability strategies, and reinforcing appropriate transition behaviors. One promising area of intervention for children with ASD is *visual support systems*. Visual supports, such as picture cues and activity schedules, may help reduce or eliminate the need for students to rely on adults to provide assistance and clarification during scheduled and unscheduled changes. Because children with ASD typically respond to visual input as their primary source of information (Quill, 1995), the use of visual support systems can supplement verbal directions when students have deficits in auditory processing. In addition, children with ASD may prefer photographs of people to the people themselves; even when directly interacting with people, these children tend to focus on physical features rather than attending to the person as an intact entity (Heflin & Alaimo, 2007).

---

### What Does the Literature Say About Activity Schedules?

Research indicates that activity schedules have been effective for students with autism spectrum disorders in the following areas:

*Transition Behaviors*

- Progressing successfully between steps in an activity (Dauphin, Kinney, & Stromer, 2004; Morrison, Sainato, Benchaaban, & Endo, 2002)
- Progressing successfully between activities (Bryan & Gast, 2000; Dooley, Wilczenski, & Torem, 2001; Hall, McClannahan, & Krantz, 1995; MacDuff, Krantz, & McClannahan, 1993; Massey & Wheeler, 2000)

*Communication Skills*

- Scripted and unscripted verbal interactions (Krantz & McClannahan, 1998)

*Daily Living Skills*

- Vocational training (Watanabe & Sturmey, 2003)
- Independent dressing (Pierce & Schreibman, 1994)
- Meal preparation (Pierce & Schreibman)

*Academics*

- Increased on-task behavior (Bryan & Gast, 2000; Massey & Wheeler, 2000; Morrison et al., 2002)

*Inappropriate Behaviors*

- Reducing tantrum behaviors (e.g., crying, screaming, aggression; Dooley et al., 2001; MacDuff et al., 1993; Krantz & McClannahan, 1993)
- Reducing noncompliance (Dettmer, Simpson, Myles, & Ganz, 2000)

---

*Activity schedules* are a promising educational strategy to support transitions for students with autism (Scheuermann & Webber, 2002; Wetherby & Prizant, 2000). An activity schedule is a visual support system that combines photographs, images, or drawings in a sequential format to represent a targeted sequence of the student's day. Activity schedules provide predictability throughout the student's day and allow a student to anticipate changes in the daily routine. Providing the student with increased time to process upcoming changes enhances the opportunity for increased participation in existing routines and transitions (Jamieson, 2004). Best of all, activity schedules are easy to construct and can be applied to existing routines in general education classrooms with minimal effort.

Researchers in a number of studies have consistently found activity schedules to be an effective intervention for children with ASD (Banda & Grimmett, 2008; see box, "What Does the Literature Say About Activity Schedules?"). Using research-based strategies not only enhances teacher efficiency but also complies with the No Child Left Behind Act of 2001's

---

**Online Resources for Activity Schedules**

http://atto.buffalo.edu/registered/ATBasics/Populations/aac/schedules.php
> This Web site is part of the Assistive Technology Training Online Project of the University of Buffalo and provides an overview of different visual support systems.

http://www.joeschedule.com/
> For a minimal fee, this Web site can help teachers plan, construct, and store their activity schedules very easily. A number of free schedules and examples are also provided.

http://autism.healingthresholds.com/therapy/visual-schedules
> This Web site provides more basic information about activity schedules, as well as a list of pertinent references.

www.mayer-johnson.com
> Mayer-Johnson is the creator of Boardmaker®, a leading picture communication symbol program.

---

directive to use evidence-based strategies. Researchers have found that activity schedule interventions can successfully reduce problem behaviors during transitions and increase daily living skills, social behavior, and social initiation in students with ASD (Banda & Grimmett; Heflin & Alaimo, 2007; Scheuermann & Webber, 2002).

Although activity schedules are frequently used by special education teachers, general education teachers can also develop and use activity schedules with students with ASD in inclusive settings. In this article, we describe steps to build activity schedules for use in general education classrooms and provide examples and resources for general education teachers (see box, "Online Resources for Activity Schedules"). By following the steps in this article and consulting with special education professionals, general education teachers will have the skills to use activity schedules to decrease transition issues in their classrooms.

## BUILDING AND IMPLEMENTING ACTIVITY SCHEDULES

### Step 1: Identify and Define Target Transition Behaviors

First, collaborate with parents and other teachers involved with the student to identify difficult transition times during the day or specific situations. Students with ASD may have problems terminating an ongoing activity or beginning a new activity. For example, a student may cry or throw materials when cleaning up the art center to transition to lunch, because the student wants to continue the current activity. Or, students may have trouble beginning a new activity, like reading, if they were not able to complete a required math worksheet. A problem behavior may also occur when a schedule is changed, even if the new activity is as desirable as the missed activity, such as a student who becomes upset when it rains and recess must be held inside.

Next, specifically describe the problem behavior. For example, "When Susie is asked to line up for lunch, she often screams 'No!' and hits the student next to her." This clearly defines the problem behavior so that any observer could identify how it relates to transition issues.

## Step 2: Collect Baseline Data on the Problem Behavior

Before introducing the activity schedule intervention, collect data on the frequency or duration of problem behaviors (e.g., refusal to complete an activity, whining, refusal to begin an activity) for 2 to 3 days to establish baseline (preintervention) data. By collecting baseline data, the teacher can determine an average frequency or duration of behavior(s) before introducing the activity schedule intervention. For dangerous or harmful behaviors, the intervention can be implemented without collecting baseline data to avoid delaying treatment.

## Step 3: Choose a Between-Activity or Within-Activity Schedule

There are two types of activity schedules: between-activity and within-activity. A between-activity schedule (see Figure 1) shows each activity of the day in order and may list the time for each activity. Students who have trouble completing multiple steps in a task analysis—for example, a student who writes her name on the paper but does not begin the assignment—may need a within-activity schedule (see Figure 2). A within-activity schedule shows the steps of a single activity in order.

## Step 4: Choose a Mode of Presentation

Activity schedules can take a number of forms, all of which can be constructed using items in the classroom. The most common mode of presentation is a simple notebook with one picture attached to each page (Bryan & Gast, 2000; Dettmer, Simpson, Myles, & Ganz, 2000). Activity schedules can also be constructed on a sentence strip by attaching Velcro and sequencing pictures. For high-functioning students in primary grades, a teacher might use multiple pictures on each page with word labels under each picture to facilitate reading skills; higher functioning students in later grades can generate their own written schedules. If the notebook is small, the student can take it from class to class to provide support throughout the day.

## Step 5: Choose a Medium for the Activity Schedule

Activity-schedule pictures can be line drawings, photos, or even lightweight objects. Pictures should be fairly simple and straightforward (see Figures 1 and 2), such as a photograph of art supplies to represent art class, and are

**Figure 1. Example of Between-Activity Schedule**

*Note.* Picture Communication Symbols © 1981–2008 by Mayer-Johnson LLC. All rights reserved world-wide. Used with permission. Boardmaker® is a registered trademark of Mayer-Johnson LLC.

readily available from commercial software (e.g., Boardmaker®, Mayer Johnson). Pictures should be selected based on the student's abilities; for a student with limited cognitive abilities, select miniature objects (e.g., small ball for play) or photographs of the student performing different activities. For higher functioning students, use abstract representations, such as clip art, line drawings, or words. The ultimate goal of the activity schedule is to increase independent transitions within and between activities and decrease problem behaviors during transition times (Bryan & Gast, 2000; Dettmer et al., 2000; Dooley, Wilczenski, & Torem, 2001; Massey & Wheeler, 2000).

## Step 6: Choose a Location for the Schedule

Attach the schedule someplace that is familiar to the child and easy to see (e.g., desk, wall, cabinet). Label the activity schedule with the child's name; have some type of container (e.g., envelope, basket, box) to hold completed activity pictures. Label each activity in words (e.g., *lunch*) to promote literacy skills and reduce dependency on pictures. Tell the student that the schedule will show him/her what to do next throughout the day. For students with portable notebooks, talk with the student to plan where to keep the notebook (e.g., desk or backpack) during each activity or class. Pages from written activity schedules can be placed into protective plastic sheets so that the student can use an overhead or dry erase marker to cross off completed steps each day.

## Step 7: Train the Student to Use the Activity Schedule

Training the student to use the activity schedule is an important step. The majority of successful interventions utilizing activity schedules use some type of training through modeling and/or prompting (Banda & Grimmett, 2008). During the training period, routinely direct the child to the activity schedule. After the completion of each activity, use verbal or physical prompts as necessary to help the student remove the picture of the completed activity, put the picture in the finished pocket/basket, and begin the next activity on the schedule. Then give praise for completing the activity and direct the student towards the next activity or step of an activity on the schedule. (For students using portable notebooks, model how to cross each step or activity off the list after it is completed.)

## Step 8: Collect Intervention Data

Continue to collect data while using the activity schedule to determine if problem behaviors are decreasing from baseline levels. Monitor data regularly to determine the effectiveness of the activity schedule strategy. The child should begin to use the schedule more independently and display fewer problem behaviors during transitions. If the strategy is not working, retrain the student using the procedure outlined in Step 7.

## Step 9: Add New Pictures or Words

When the student is able to transition within or between selected activities, even with prompts, extend the use of the activity schedule to cover a longer period of time within the same setting or subject. For example, if a student uses an activity schedule to complete an independent writing activity, add steps to guide the student to complete the subsequent small-group writing activity. This way, more pictures or words can be added as the student begins using the activity schedules independently.

## Step 10: Fade Prompts

As a student becomes more independent in the use of the schedule, reduce prompting. If a student does not respond to a class-wide request to begin the next activity, individually address the student and announce the next activity. This type of cue will help the child focus on the next activity rather than allowing his refusal to escalate into a tantrum. Gradually provide fewer physical and verbal prompts until the student is able to independently complete an activity, check the schedule, move the

**Figure 2. Example of Within-Activity Schedule**

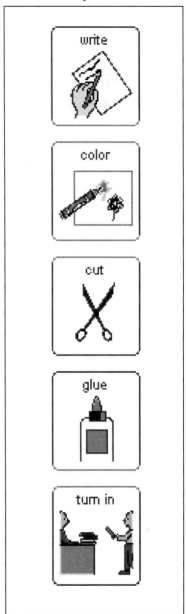

*Note.* Picture Communication Symbols © 1981–2008 by Mayer-Johnson LLC. All rights reserved worldwide. Used with permission. Boardmaker® is a trademark of Mayer-Johnson LLC.

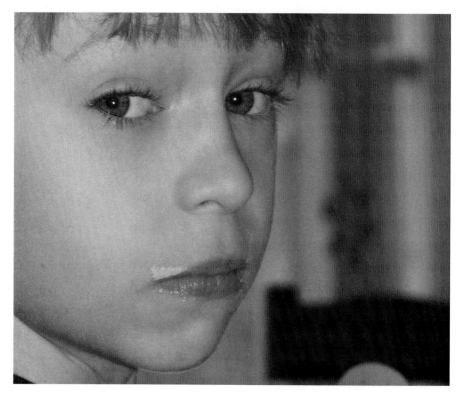

activity picture from the schedule to "finished" box, and transition to the next activity. For higher functioning students or those using portable notebooks, independent use of an activity schedule should require minimal verbal or non-verbal adult prompts, such as a gesture towards the notebook.

## Step 11: Fade the Prominence of the Activity Schedule

This step is intended to make the schedule both socially and age appropriate. Move the schedule from the wall into a binder and discontinue using Velcro. Put all of the pictures into a one-page document and have the student check or cross off each item as it is completed. Shrink the size of the pictures and increase the size of the words until the schedule uses words only. When the student no longer needs to physically check off each item, remove the binder. The schedule can be laminated and attached to the student's desk.

Finally, shrink the size of the text, print, and laminate the schedule so that it can be folded to fit in a wallet or purse. At this point, the schedule is essentially a list of activities. "Pocket" schedules can be continued into the teenage and adult years.

## Step 12: Promote Generalization Across Activities and Settings

Apply activity schedules to transitions in as many settings as possible. As the student learns to use the activity schedule, steps for additional activities may be added to increase the student's level of independence. For example, being able to complete a sequence of "name on paper, color, cut, glue, and turn in" to complete a vocabulary worksheet suggests the student may be ready to use an activity schedule to follow steps in a math activity. The strength of activity schedules is the ease in which they can be planned, constructed, and incorporated into existing activities across a number of settings. Following initial training, children with ASD can use activity schedules to independently complete complex tasks and remain engaged in a variety of settings and situations (MacDuff, Krantz, & McClannahan, 1993). Home-based activity schedules may be implemented to increase participation in leisure activities, social interaction, self-care, and housekeeping tasks (Krantz, MacDuff, & McClannahan, 1993).

## FINAL THOUGHTS

Activity schedules have been shown to be effective interventions for students with ASD, and can be considered an evidence-based teaching strategy that may help students transition more easily between scheduled routines and activities. Activity schedules also have shown promise in teaching on-task behaviors and can serve as a valuable support in helping students with ASD manage the multiple tasks typically found in inclusive settings. By following the steps presented in this article, general education teachers can plan and construct activity schedules to meet the needs of individual students with ASD.

## REFERENCES

American Psychiatric Association. (2000). *Diagnostic and statistical manual of mental disorders* (4th ed. rev.). Washington, DC: Author.

Banda, D. R., & Grimmett, E. (2008). Enhancing social and transition behaviors of persons with autism through activity schedules: A review. *Education and Training in Developmental Disabilities, 43,* 324–333.

Bryan, L. C., & Gast, D. L. (2000). Teaching on-task and on-schedule behaviors to high-functioning children with autism via picture activity schedules. *Journal of Autism and Developmental Disorders, 30,* 553–567.

Centers for Disease Control and Prevention. (2007, February 9). *CDC releases new data on autism spectrum disorders (ASD) from multiple communities in the United States* [Press release]. Retrieved February 22, 2007, from http://www.cdc.gov/od/oc/media/pressrel/2007/r070208.htm

Dauphin, M., Kinney, E. M., & Stromer, R. (2004). Using video-enhanced activity schedules and matrix training to teach sociodramatic play to a child with autism. *Journal of Positive Behavior Interventions, 6,* 238–250.

Dettmer, S., Simpson, R. L., Myles, B. S., & Ganz, J. B. (2000). The use of visual supports to facilitate transitions of students with autism. *Focus on Autism and Other Developmental Disabilities, 15,* 163–169.

Dooley, P., Wilczenski, F. L., & Torem, C. (2001). Using an activity schedule to smooth school transitions. *Journal of Positive Behavior Interventions, 3*, 57–61.

Forest, E. J., Horner, R. H., Lewis-Palmer, T., & Todd, A. W. (2004). Transitions for young children with autism from preschool to kindergarten. *Journal of Positive Behavior Interactions, 6*, 103–112.

Hall, L. J., McClannahan, L. E., & Krantz, P. J. (1995). Promoting independence in integrated classrooms by teaching aides to use activity schedules and decreased prompts. *Education and Training in Mental Retardation and Developmental Disabilities, 30*, 208–217.

Heflin, L. J., & Alaimo, D. F. (2007). *Students with autism spectrum disorders: Effective instructional practices.* Upper Saddle River, NJ: Pearson Education.

Jamieson, S. (2004). Creating an educational program for young children who are blind and who have autism. *RE:view, 35*, 165–177.

Krantz, P. J., MacDuff, M. T., & McClannahan, L. E. (1993). Programming participation in family activities for children with autism: Parents' use of photographic activity schedules. *Journal of Applied Behavior Analysis, 26*(1), 137–138.

Krantz, P. J., & McClannahan, L. E. (1993). Teaching children with autism to initiate to peers: Effects of script-fading procedure. *Journal of Applied Behavior Analysis, 26*, 121–132.

Krantz, P. J., & McClannahan, L. E. (1998). Social interaction skills for children with autism: A script-fading procedure for beginning readers. *Journal of Applied Behavior Analysis, 31*, 191–202.

MacDuff, G. S., Krantz, P. J., & McClannahan, L. E. (1993). Teaching children with autism to use photographic activity schedules: Maintenance and generalization of complex response chains. *Journal of Applied Behavior Analysis, 26*, 89–97.

Massey, N. G., & Wheeler, J. J. (2000). Acquisition and generalization of activity schedules and their effects on task management in a young child with autism in an inclusive pre-school classroom. *Education and Training in Mental Retardation and Developmental Disabilities, 35*, 326–335.

Morrison, R. S., Sainato, D. M., Benchaaban, D., & Endo, S. (2002). Increasing play skills of children with autism using activity schedules and correspondence training. *Journal of Early Intervention, 25*, 58–72.

Pierce, K. L., & Schreibman, L. (1994). Teaching daily living skills to children with autism in unsupervised settings through pictorial self-management. *Journal of Applied Behavior Analysis, 27*, 471–481.

Quill, K. A. (1995). Visually cued instruction for children with autism and pervasive developmental disorders. *Focus on Autistic Behavior, 10*, 10-20.

Scheuermann, B., & Webber, J. (2002). *Autism: Teaching DOES make a difference.* Belmont, CA: Wadsworth-Thomson Learning.

Schreibman, L., Whalen, C., & Stahmer, A. (2000). The use of video priming to reduce disruptive transition behavior in children with autism. *Journal of Positive Behavior Interventions, 2*, 3–11.

Watanabe, M., & Sturmey, P. (2003). The effect of choice-making opportunities during activity schedules on task engagement of adults with autism. *Journal of Autism and Developmental Disorders, 33*, 535–538.

Wetherby, A. M., & Prizant, B. M. (2000). *Autism spectrum disorders: A transactional developmental perspective.* Baltimore: Paul H. Brookes.

Originally published in *TEACHING Exceptional Children*, Vol. 41, No. 4, pp. 16–21.